Trogons

of the

Arizona Borderlands

by

Richard Cachor Taylor

Drawings by Kathryn McLane

Published by
Treasure Chest Publications, Inc.
P.O. Box 5250
Tucson AZ 85703-0250

Design and typesetting by
Casa Cold Type, Inc.

Cover design by
Lynn Bishop Graphics

Front cover: Male Elegant Trogon
Photograph by Greg R. Homel, Natural Elements Photo-Research

Back cover: Female Elegant Trogon
Photograph by Greg R. Homel, Natural Elements Photo-Research

Printed in the U.S.A.
Printing 10 9 8 7 6 5 4 3 2 1

ISBN 0-918080-78-9

Contents

The Eared Trogon in Arizona

Acknowledgments

I am deeply indebted to artist Kathryn McLane, whose two-year stay in the Chiricahua Mountains is reflected in her sensitive drawings of both the trogon and its world.

I am indebted to the following people who freely shared their information and their ideas while I researched the section on the Eared Trogon: John Bates, Gale Monson, Robert J. Morse, Rose Ann Rowlett, Alexander Skutch, Robert T. Smith, Helen Snyder, Sally and Walter Spofford, Lynne Taylor, Sheri Williamson, Tom Wood, and Dale A. Zimmerman.

Among others to whom I owe thanks: Alexander Clay, Jim des Lauriers, William A. Davis, John Epler, Ralph A. Fisher, Jr., Bill Harrison, Alden Hayes, Kim Innes, Kenn Kaufman, Nancy Manning, Bettina Martin, Charles W. McMoran, G. Scott Mills, Gale Monson, Ruth Morse, Sam Negri, Joan and Carroll Peabody, Sue Perger, Barbara and Vince Roth, and Stephen M. Russell.

I would also like to express my appreciation to the memberships of the Huachuca, Maricopa, Southwestern New Mexico, and Tucson Audubon Societies, and to the wildlife staff of the Coronado National Forest for their field time and interest in the conservation of the Elegant Trogon.

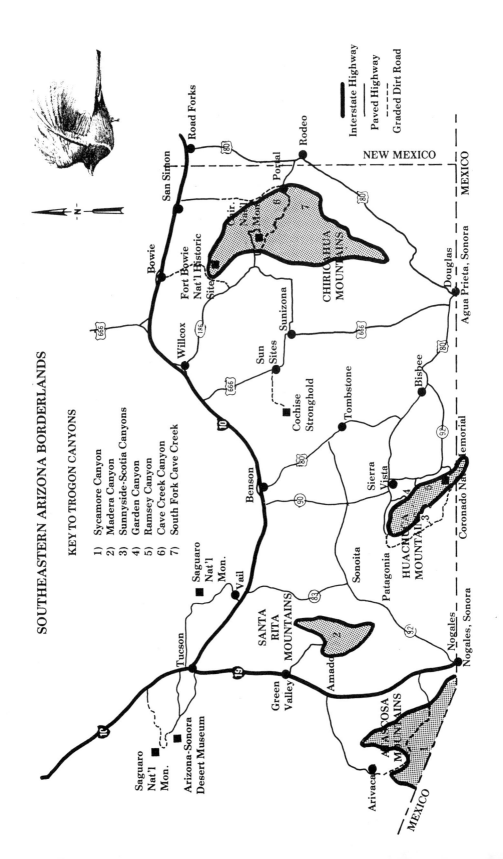

SOUTHEASTERN ARIZONA BORDERLANDS

KEY TO TROGON CANYONS

1) Sycamore Canyon
2) Madera Canyon
3) Sunnyside-Scotia Canyons
4) Garden Canyon
5) Ramsey Canyon
6) Cave Creek Canyon
7) South Fork Cave Creek

Interstate Highway
Paved Highway
Graded Dirt Road

NEW MEXICO

MEXICO

Road Forks

Rodeo

Portal

San Simon

Bowie

Fort Bowie
Nat'l Historic
Site

Willcox

Sunizona

Sun
Sites

Cochise
Stronghold

Tombstone

Benson

Vail

Saguaro
Nat'l
Mon.

Tucson

Saguaro
Nat'l
Mon.

Arizona-Sonora
Desert Museum

Green
Valley

SANTA
RITA
MOUNTAINS

Amado

Sonoita

Patagonia

Nogales
Nogales, Sonora

Sierra
Vista

HUACHUCA
MOUNTAINS

Coronado Nat'l Memorial

Bisbee

Douglas

Agua Prieta, Sonora

CHIRICAHUA
MOUNTAINS

ATASCOSA
MOUNTAINS

Arivaca

MEXICO

The Elegant Trogon
in Arizona

I

Introduction

On a muggy day in mid-July, 1976, I witnessed a pair of Elegant Trogons defending their nest against a marauding Sonora Gopher Snake.

Fully five feet long, the reptile was twice its length up the chalk white column of a sycamore tree. The chiming, food-begging calls of the young betrayed the dark entrance of the nest cavity not far above. While the snake cautiously tested each crevice and wart of the bark's slick surface before inching upwards, both adult trogons were motionless, churring their distress in a series of hoarse, rapid *chucks*. The male held a large, green larva in its bill. Occasionally he readjusted this tidbit, obviously meant for the nestlings. After 20 minutes, he finally swallowed the caterpillar. The spell was broken.

With powerful wing beats, it closed the short gap separating perch from gopher snake, balancing its brilliant body on a vertical axis. Before the snake could react, the bird battered its upper torso with a flurry of stiff-edged wing blows.

Now it was the female trogon's turn. Repeatedly, with no further assistance from her mate, she hovered within inches of the serpent's head, drumming the air and diving bill-first at the nest assailant.

For at least five minutes the reptile held its position, only weaving its blunt head and flicking a black tongue. Then, as the female attacked yet again, it lunged. She avoided the strike by a wide margin. Down the smooth, white trunk slid the snake in a rasping, slow-motion fall. And then silence. A tableau unbroken even by the young, who must have felt the danger telegraphed up through the decaying tree.

After a minute, I walked over to where the gopher snake lay collapsed at the foot of the sycamore. It seemed stunned or dead. I extended my boot to touch it; the snake nailed my toe in a lightning-swift stroke, coiled and began vibrating its tail in the leaves. With newborn respect, I looked again to where the trogons perched facing me, clearly alarmed, yet not willing to quit. Then I drove the reptile away from the nest vicinity.

There is a land of mystery along the border in Southeastern Arizona. Here, a handful of rugged, blue ranges, outliers of the Mexican Plateau, rise sharply from the desert and support islands of plant and animal life drawn from both the Rocky Mountains and the Sierra Madres. Ecological boundaries are in solution here, with a constant influx of species, temperate and tropical. Together they create the richest land-bounded community of wildlife found within the whole of the United States.

The most eloquent symbol of the Arizona-Sonora borderland is the Elegant Trogon.

Scarlet-red breast, smoke-gray wing, emerald-green body, all fuse with a long metallic tail in the male to form a foot-long bird of molten beauty. A lemon-yellow bill and an orange eye-ring set off the large, dark pupil.

Female trogons are dove-gray in body with resplendent coppery tails and rose-red bellies. White encircles her eye, enclosing an inner pencil-line of orange. Staining each cheek is a distinctive small, white "teardrop," broadly shaped like the letter "Z." Both sexes alike have a white breast band, and an undertail laddered with alternating black and white bars.

Trogons are rare. Found breeding only in Southeastern Arizona within the U.S., fewer than 50 pairs occupy an area of over 10,000 square miles. Yet, so limited are they in their choice of habitat, that the knowledgeable can predict, almost to the acre, where trogons are likely to summer. Because they use the deep, well-watered canyons that form an ecological bridge joining timbered mountain highland to hot desert floor, trogons share their environment with a host of other rare U.S. birds, mammals, and reptiles. Because they are low in number, yet highly visible, Elegant Trogons are a sensitive barometer to the biotic health of Arizona's borderland canyons.

The abundance—or absence—of Elegant Trogons in the mountains of Southeastern Arizona will tell our future generations exactly how well we managed the land.

II
Early History

Range Expansion

On September 20, 1884, a laborer in the Santa Catalina Mountains saw what he took for "a kind of bird of paradise." His description of the spectacular plumage was precise enough to enable pioneer ornithologist W. E. D. Scott to publish his sighting as the first recorded occurrence of the Elegant Trogon in Arizona. Less than a year later, on August 24, 1885, a specimen of *Trogon elegans* was collected near Fort Huachuca by an off-duty Army officer. Pausing in the midst of the United States campaign to subdue the Chiricahua Apache Indian nation, Lieutenant H. C. Benson established forever more that trogons could be found north of the international boundary.

Were these the first trogons to cross the border separating the U.S. from Sonora, or had they long been a casual member of Arizona's avifauna? I believe the trogons reported by Scott and Benson represented the advance wave of a northern range expansion. Four species of reasoning support that conclusion.

Fossils: There is no paleontological or archaeological evidence that any form of trogon ever occurred in Arizona prior to recent times. The trogon family was well known to Mexico's Indians, and the Resplendent Quetzal—its largest member—held a sacred position in their pantheon. Scarlet Macaw and the Thick-billed Parrot are among the bird skeletons associated with Arizona's prehistoric villages, but no trogon remains have ever been discovered.

Dr. Emil Haury, President Emeritus of the Arizona State Museum, has stated that the Elegant Trogon appears to be just one example of a neotropical species that extended its range northwards around the turn of the century. The coati, a long-nosed, long-tailed relative of the raccoon, is apparently another. Immigrant coatis were first spotted in the Huachuca Mountains in 1892, and they were not reported from the Chiricahuas until 1929.

History: Southeastern Arizona, part of the Gadsden Purchase in 1853, gained early recognition as a biological treasure trove among Eastern scientists. Two of those who explored the island-like mountain ranges in the arid heart of Apacheria were Dr. Elliot Coues and Harry W. Henshaw. During the 1860s and 1870s, they described many new avian species from this area. Some of their discoveries—the Broad-billed Hummingbird, Buff-breasted Flycatcher, Sulphur-bellied Flycatcher, and the Strickland's Woodpecker, for example—share the Elegant Trogon's habitat in Arizona.

It seems improbable that such competent observers, working in the right canyons at the correct time of year, would have overlooked the single bird with the most conspicuous voice and plumage found along the U.S.-Mexico border, had it been present.

Trogon Behavior: From Scott's second-hand description of the "bird of paradise," it appears the first trogon seen in Arizona was a female. Lieutenant Benson's trophy skin belonged to an immature male. Northern post-breeding season wandering is characteristic of female and immature Elegant Trogons. In September 1977, a female was photographed on the Rio Grande River in Texas, about 100 miles north of the nearest breeding population in Mexico. Similarly, Arizona's northernmost record is of a female killed by a curious prospector near the Verde River on October 21, 1976. This trogon was nearly 200 miles out of range. An immature male found near Tucson in January 1953 became Arizona's first record of a winter Elegant.

It is important to note that both female and immature trogons are somberly colored in comparison to the gorgeous red and green hues of the adult male bird. Moreover, all age

Coati, first discovered in Arizona in 1892

and sex groups of trogons are almost entirely silent in the fall and winter. I feel the first two records of trogons in Arizona stand as a tribute to the sensitivity of Scott's laborer and to Lieutenant Benson. Trogons are not easy to find after mid-August.

__Known Dispersal Rate:__ Finally, the after-the-fact argument: apparently the modern range expansion of the Elegant Trogon into Arizona has taken place over decades, by inches, not by leagues. A 25-mile-long isthmus of oak woodland connects the Santa Rita to the Huachuca Mountains. Yet, it was not until 1918 that A. B. Howell first observed trogons in this ornithologist's paradise, fully 33 years after Benson's bird was reported from the Huachucas.

Some 54 years elapsed before Dave Brown and Ron Anderson of the Arizona Game and Fish Department found *T. elegans* across the Santa Cruz River Valley in the Atascosa highlands in 1972. The airline distance separating habitat pockets in the Atascosas from the Santa Ritas is approximately 25 miles.

Today, the largest canyon population of Elegant Trogons in the U.S. is found in the strawberry-walled Cave Creek drainage on the eastern flank of the Chiricahua Mountains. Although only 50 miles from the San Luis Range of the Sierra Madre Occidental—where a nesting female was collected in 1892—no trogon was sighted in Cave Creek for another 50 years. Alden Hayes, now retired from the National Park Service, saw the first bird near the "old orchard" at Portal in 1942.

The lack of specimens does not reflect lack of scientific interest in Cave Creek Canyon. J. Eugene Law, with the assistance of A. J. van Rossem and others, made a definitive collection of Chiricahua avifauna from 1913 to 1921. Apparently, no trogons were present; no records or skins exist from Law's expeditions.

At this remove in time, it is impossible to state uncategorically that the Elegant Trogon's romance with Arizona only began a century ago. Still, the data I have fits that assumption. Even our knowledge about this area's climate. James Hastings and Raymond Turner, in a study of changing vegetation patterns, conclude that "Mean annual temperatures in Arizona may have risen by 3 or 3.5 degrees F. since the 1870s." Enough, perhaps, to create a niche for a new Sierra Madrean bird on Arizona's southern frontier.

Population Growth

The slow dispersal of trogons into the four major mountain groups along the Arizona-Sonora border can, in part, be attributed to their low reproductive potential. Elegant Trogons only lay two eggs in the average clutch. Barely half of all Cave Creek Canyon nests I have watched successfully fledge young. And, since many of these probably do not survive to maturity, it is evident that many seasons are required to establish a new trogon population through natural propagation. Wandering Mexican "spill-over" birds are probably not an important factor: the rate of their range expansion in Arizona suggests pairs of Elegants seldom gamble reproductive success on habitat islands they've never explored.

Humankind, too, probably played an important role in retarding trogon dispersal. Early ornithology was steeped in blood. A shotgun was deemed more indispensable to the practitioner than a pair of binoculars.

Between 1892 and 1902, bird historians A.C. Bent and Harry S. Swarth record the deaths of six trogons, all from the Huachucas; very probably other birds were shot without documentation. John C. MacIntyre, the last survivor of an 1890s religious commune in Sunnyside Canyon of the Huachuca Mountains, recalled that Frank C. Willard offered the village boys 50 cents apiece for trogon eggs. That no boy ever collected this princely bounty is convincing proof of the trogon's scarcity at the turn of the century.

But Elegant Trogons were establishing roots in the United States in spite of human harassment. Howell described the first pair of trogons to be seen in the Santa Rita Mountains as already gun "wise." By 1932, wrote van Rossem, there were eight trogons in Madera Canyon. Van Rossem then subtracted a male and an immature from Madera's total. Skins in the University of Arizona's collection and published accounts by Herbert W. Brandt, a collector, show that by the 1930s trogons were present in nearly all of the Huachuca's south-facing canyons.

Although protected by law in 1929, interest in Arizona's trogons continued to express itself primarily through the medium of birdshot until 1939. In 1939, Dr. Arthur A. Allen discovered the first nest of the Elegant Trogon in the United States.

The First Nest

Probably the single greatest roadblock between the trogon and a birder ethos that would prevent man-caused nest disturbances is the *macho* behavior of some male birds. These individuals select territories in the same shady groves of sycamores that man covets for campgrounds, perhaps for many of the same reasons. With unforgettable aggressive displays of crimson red breast and continuous loud calls, the male challenges all intruders and, ironically, advertises the presence of a nearby nest hole. Birdwatchers of every stripe, including listers, photographers, and tour guides, are attracted to the locality as the fame of the "tame" trogon spreads. And finally, in most cases, the burden of human attention leads to nest abandonment.

But occasionally the male adjusts to every quantum jump in birdwatcher attention. Arthur A. Allen must have found such a bird in Madera Canyon in the summer of 1939.

Dr. Allen, a professor of ornithology at Cornell University, was touring the U.S. with both a camera and a tape recorder when he learned about the trogon from Roger Tory Peterson. Peterson, in his turn, had been shown the trogon earlier by another famous bird artist, Allen Brooks. When "Doc" Allen arrived in the Santa Rita Mountains, he was personally escorted to the bird's territory by Dr. Charles T. Vorhies of the University of Arizona. Within a few hours, he did what no one else had done since the discovery of the Elegant Trogon in Arizona 55 years earlier: Arthur Allen found a nest.

> A flutter of wings close behind me, and a low, growling call. Quickly I turned and nearly slipped from my precarious perch when my gaze fell upon the crimson breast and iridescent green head of an Elegant Trogon. It was less than 10 feet from my incredulous eye . . .

> The next day, with the aid of a mirror and a flashlight, we settled the great question, for there, 14 inches down from the opening and with no sign of nesting material, were two shiny-white eggs.

Doc Allen neither shot the birds nor collected their eggs. Instead of feathers, he took photographs and tapes. When the narrative of Allen's discovery was published in the June 1944 issue of *National Geographic Magazine,* it launched a new era in human-trogon relations. Today, trogon appreciation probably accounts for 25,000 annual visits to the canyons of the Arizona borderlands.

III

The Most Elegant Bird in North America

The Name

*T*rogons belong to a pan-tropical family of birds encompassing 35 members distinguished by their richly colored, iridescent plumage. Taxonomically, the trogons exhibit two characters shared by no other groups. Like parrots and most woodpeckers, trogons have two of their four toes pointing backward; but, in the trogons, it is the first and second digits—instead of the first and fourth, a condition known as heterodactyl. And North American trogons, excluding the Resplendent Quetzal and Eared Trogon, have a serrated edge on the upper mandible. *Trogonurus*, a Greek root, translates to "the one who gnaws," and commemorates their saw-tooth bill.

The ancestral family line can be traced back 30 to 40 million years to *Archaeotrogon* in the humid forests of what is present-day France. Of all the living species, ranging from the 14-inch-long Quetzal with its magnificent three-foot-long tail coverts to the diminutive eight-inch-long Violaceous Trogon, Arizona's representative falls within the medium-size class. Elegant Trogons are 11 to 12 inches in overall length and weigh 65 to 75 grams—or about as much as a man's wristwatch. Although the sexes overlap in size, females tend to be slightly larger than their mates, perhaps half an inch on the average. Males generally have bigger bills—a single millimeter bigger.

Arizona trogons belong to the subspecies *ambiguous*, a northern, migratory form in which the wing chord, tail length, and overall dimensions are typically one-half to one inch greater than for resident populations of *Trogon elegans* from Sinaloa, Mexico to Guanacaste, Costa Rica. Based on size and subtle plumage distinctions, the Coppery-tailed Trogon was regarded as a separate species from 1835 to 1956, when it was "lumped" with the southern Elegant Trogon.

In 1983, the name Coppery-tailed Trogon was officially changed to Elegant Trogon by the American Ornithological Union. Frequently the modifier "Elegant" fails to describe the bird. Trogons assume a pigeon-like posture at rest that I refer to in my notes as "hump-backed." Relaxing Eared Trogons and even Resplendent Quetzals adopt the exact same pose, which can really only be described as awkward-looking.

All trogons, regardless of species, can be elegant, just as they are all beautiful, all gorgeous, and possibly all hump-backed when resting. "Coppery-tailed" denoted a physical trait peculiar to this species alone, one shared by no other member of the trogon tribe. With a dutiful nod to the Law of Priority that, at least in theory, guided the A.O.U. Checklist naming committee, it's a shame that the descriptive name Coppery-tailed was changed in favor of a purely subjective adjective.

An Elegant Trogon truly is an elegant bird. I believe the adult male is both the most beautiful and the most elegant of all the birds of North America. Aesthetics, however, are a matter of personal taste, and I know others who value the size, flight, or song of another species above the color and form of the Elegant Trogon.

Male

Adult male Elegant Trogons display nine distinct colors: horn *brown* feet, *yellow* bill, *orange* eye-ring, emerald *green* back and throat, *white* breast bar and undertail, *black* face and bars on the undertail, *red* breast, smoke *gray* wing, and a metallic *copper* or olive green upper tail surface, depending on the light. A tenth hue transforms the back of the male from iridescent green to

Adult male and female Coppery-tailed Trogons

sparkling azure blue when the angle of refracted sunlight changes. The green we see on the throat, back, and crown of the head of male birds is actually a structural color, not a pigment.

I'll never forget the first male contour feather I ever found. As I held my find under the light, the pigeon-gray matrix ignited and formed three shifting, iridescent color bands: violet blue near the tip, metallic emerald, and—unexpectedly—molten gold. Perhaps it is this golden patina, never really visible under field conditions, but nonetheless present, that gives the male trogon his aura of nobility. A trogon in the sun definitely seems larger than a trogon in the shade.

Female

Plumage of female Elegant Trogons is far more somber than that of the male. Her overall body color is medium gray rinsed lightly with neutral brown. Below the off-white breast band, the feathers are tinted a soft shade of "coffee-with-cream." White encircles the eye with an oval ring, and just behind and below is the milky white tearspot. Actually, the tear marking is upside down—it comes to a point at the bottom like the punctuation for an apostrophe.

Female trogon lower bellies are a pink red, a rose petal red. In contrast to the wavy, finely sketched, charcoal lines that characterize the undertails of adult males, female trogons have boldly laddered undertails with thick, black bars. When either sex fans the tail in flight, it flashes snowy, dazzling white. The outer eight tail feathers, or rectrices, are actually translucent— outspread they trap the light like wind-blown linen.

It is the female that formerly gave the species its best claim to the name "Coppery-tailed." I have seen the tail of the same male bird change from dull copper to a cupreous green as it shifted perches. But even under poor light conditions, the female trogon's tail is a rich, coppery brown; seen in strong sun, the inner four rectrices of her tail reflect like priceless, polished metal. The tails of all males are broadly tipped with ink black; the posterior surface of the female tail is, in most cases, a long, clean blade ending without emargination. And, of all the trogon dimensions, the female's tail is most likely to exceed that of her mate.

Fledgling

The plumage of a new fledgling is adapted for camouflage. Head and throat are a muddy gray-brown, and the overall head silhouette is broken by an oval, white eye-ring and an off-white teardrop on the cheek. The cream-colored breast band is not well-defined where it merges with the mottled gray breast and abdomen. Wings manifest disruptive coloration again, with three rows of lightly yellowed spots traversing the coverts on the shoulders. By disguising the outline of the bird, disruptive coloration probably helps protect the young trogon from predation.

Only the back is not a dull, neutral tone. Here the fledgling's contour feathers are a warm, lustrous brown, undoubtedly useful for the parent birds in tracing their line of flight. Yet once the young assumes a shady perch, the telltale shimmer disappears.

Fledglings leave the nest cavity with tails only two inches grown, less than one-third of adult length. Topside, the tails appear a dark, business-suit brown; beneath, they are trimmed white with a crisp, black wedge of rectrices clearly visible in the center.

Weight-wise, the new fledgling is just under 50 grams—or about two-thirds of adult size. But growth is rapid. One month out of the nest, immatures are fully adult in all dimensions. At this stage in their development, sometime between July and September, they are apt to be mistaken for mature females, since they have a tearspot behind the eye and a heavily barred undertail. But the wingspots and the mottled breasts still persist.

It is now that sexual dimorphism in plumage begins to show. Male trogons exchange faded back feathers for brilliant green. Females molt into a fresh shade of cinnamon. The transformation first appears at the base of the tail in both sexes, and, over the course of their second month out of the nest, it spreads gradually upwards to the crown of the head. Meantime, both sexes alike are acquiring bright, apple-red abdomens. This is the last plumage young birds exhibit before they migrate out of Arizona for the winter.

Molt

The most comical of the Arizona trogon plumages is the tailless adult female. During the course of incubation, her seven-inch-long tail suffers considerable abrasion. Nest holes average only

5½ inches in diameter, and trogons enter and leave head-first. If her tail is tattered by the time the eggs hatch, three weeks later, it's in rags. Then comes the August molt. It is not uncommon for females to lose their tails entirely.

Imagine a six-inch-long bird—including a blunt, inch-long-tail—with wings projecting so far beyond the body they look like they're dragging. Color the bird mouse gray and attach a heavy, saw-toothed bill. Remember: don't laugh! Three weeks later, her new copper rectrices have grown out again.

I have never seen an adult male trogon similarly inconvenienced, but bird-of-the-year males have an awkward adolescent plumage stage when they look half and half of each sex. Throat and back are gleaming green; the eye-ring, however, is only faint orange, and there may still be a shadowy tearspot. Its breast is bright red, although distinctly split in the center with white—like a velvet vest over a cheap T-shirt. And the undertail is still heavily cross-barred, just like a female's. Such are the tribulations of the young male.

Elegant Trogons lend themselves to this kind of anthropomorphism by virtue of their anatomy. It's natural to ascribe human traits to them. Unlike most families of birds, which assume a horizontal posture when perched, trogons sit upright after the fashion of hawks and eagles. Like the birds of prey, trogons have large, dark eyes and down-curved bills. These two features give trogons a "face," and the face, in turn, seems to confer upon trogons the ability to think and feel emotions.

Their overall man-like appearance is reinforced by a long tail, proportional to legs, which is clearly divided into twin feather tracts. The tail flares basally. Because trogons have exceptionally short tarsi, usually buried deep in feathers, and small, inconspicuous feet, nothing allays the leg-like impression created by each rectrix.

No wonder, then, that Middle American Indians felt that Resplendent Quetzals represented the reincarnated souls of their warriors. It would be interesting to know the subconscious motivations that bring people to Southeastern Arizona to see the Elegant Trogon.

IV

Trogon Dynamics: The Physical Powers

*E*legant Trogons are medium-sized birds in the world of the Arizona pine-oak woodland. They are larger than wrens, titmice, warblers, flycatchers, towhees, orioles, and tanagers. They are smaller than the bird predators, such as Sharp-shinned Hawks, Cooper's Hawks, Northern Goshawks, Prairie and Peregrine Falcons. Trogons are in the same size league with Gray-breasted Jays, Northern Flickers and American Robins. All three of these species outweigh the Elegant Trogon, but that may not be apparent to even the birds themselves. Trogons have extremely deep, dense plumage. And overall they are an inch or so longer.

Wings

Elegant Trogons have a total wingspan of approximately one foot. Their bantam weight proves an advantage here, enabling them to actually hover for several seconds as they snatch arthropods and small fruits from the crown foliage of trees and shrubs. After capturing the prey item, they usually rise buoyantly to a nearby perch, easily shrugging off the effects of gravity. Only hummingbirds exercise greater aerial control.

In Arizona, there is considerable dietary overlap with Gray-breasted Jays and American Robins for the larvae, cicadas, and canyon grapes which constitute important staples of the trogon food supply at different seasons of the year. Most interspecific competition is avoided, however, because neither of these two heavier opportunists is equipped for taking food from the outermost twigs. No other pine-oak woodland bird, which eats large insects or berries, is capable of duplicating the trogon's foraging mode.

Trogons manifest their extraordinary flight powers in other arenas as well. Nest exits are predictably explosive. One moment the trogon is surveying its domain, head and torso encapsulated in the nest chamber; the next, the bird shoots off at maximum velocity. There is absolutely no detectable point at which acceleration began.

Generally, trogons depart from their nests on a horizontal plane. More remarkable, they lift directly out of bathing pools on a vertical trajectory. Relatively few species of birds in the world, terrestrial or aquatic, can rocket straight up out of a pool, trailing a column of water behind.

But no member of the trogon family is known as a particularly strong flier. With deeply rounded, concave wings, the Elegant is not an exception. I once had the opportunity to clock an adult female on my pickup truck speedometer as she flew down the Cave Creek Canyon Road in the Chiricahua Mountains. Her speed over a 50-yard course was approximately 20 miles per hour. Trogons probably do fly faster in short bursts, but they belong among the slower birds when it comes to distance. Trailing long, rudder-like tails, trogons are designed for acrobatics, not marathons.

Band-tailed Pigeons take off with great, thunderous claps. Gray-breasted Jays create a noise like air blowing over a hollow bottle as they fly. Far more subtle, the undulatory flight of the Elegant Trogon sounds like a flag whipping on a stiff wind—if you are close enough.

I found the last trogon I saw in South Fork Cave Creek in 1979 by hearing it first. The bird, a young male of the year, was feeding in a Canyon Grape vine overhanging the trail just 30 feet behind me. I was watching the last Painted Redstart and Hepatic Tanager of the failing summer, hot colors flitting

Nestling trogon, waiting to be fed

through dying leaves. All around, American Robins were calling jealously, dashing from one perch to another. I really don't know how long it took before I filtered out the sound of the foraging trogon. I was surprised, but I was ready the next time it flew.

The tail fanned out for balance, striking white, as it hovered briefly to seize a berry. Then the bird jetted to a nearby perch in an emerald streak. I suppose I could have stayed to take more notes. But I left before anything or anyone else could sully the purity of the moment.

Legs and Feet

The legs of the Elegant Trogon are short. Natural selection has apparently reduced them to the minimum necessary for perching and for climbing in and out of nest holes. As a bird which feeds at a hover—the form of flight that consumes the most energy—bone amounts to unwanted ballast. The trogon family is characterized world-over by small tarsi and little feet. But, unlike hummingbirds, Elegant Trogons can walk. Territorial encounters between two males may well terminate with a session on the ground, or on a broad, low limb. Breasts pumped up in an angry display of scarlet, males sidle towards each other in tiny, mincing steps, uttering low calls and snapping bills. Curiously, the males advance on one another sideways, moving crabwise. Footing seems to play a crucial role: sometimes the dominant bird will fly off first, immediately taking a nearby position where the turf is apparently more to its liking.

Trogons of both sexes are excellent climbers. After two weeks, even the nestlings can scale the vertical walls of their nursery, usually an abandoned woodpecker hole. By the time they fledge three to 10 days later, the young scamper up the shaft to be fed by their parents.

Nestling trogons share a unique adaptation with the juveniles of other cavity dwelling families that do not line their nests. Like woodpeckers and kingfishers, baby trogons have heel pads to help elevate their featherless bodies off the bare floor of the hole.

For two years of my study, I watched a one-footed male trogon in South Fork Cave Creek of the Chiricahua Mountains. Both years, this bird secured a mate and a territory. But both years were tempered with mortality. In 1978, a predator got the eggs after two weeks of incubation; 1979 saw the loss of his mate after it inexplicably developed a large tumor on the back of its head. Even without the female's help, however, Peg-leg fledged one young.

That a crippled trogon is capable of successfully breeding underscores a paradox. Obviously, trogons are equipped with strong tarsi if a one-footed bird can ascend a perpendicular tube two times a day during incubation, 20 or more times a day during the first fortnight of nestling feeding. But the success of this male illustrates just how unimportant two healthy legs and feet really are in the overall ecology of the Elegant Trogon. A bad wing would mean certain death for any trogon.

Bill

Bird bills often tell us more about how a species makes its living than any other single feature. Bills represent the most adaptable point of contact between a bird and its surrounding environment. The bill of an Elegant Trogon is short, broad, stout and saw-toothed. There is a hook on the upper mandible.

The tendency for female trogons to have a slight size advantage over their mates is reversed in the case of the bill. Male culmen measurements average 18.2 millimeters, females 17.2, a difference favoring the cock by a fraction over five percent.

In some species, such as the Strickland's Woodpecker where the male's bill is substantially larger than the female's, each sex prefers a slightly different foraging substrate. This reduces competition for food between the pair and enables them to better exploit a smaller territory. In the world of *T. elegans*, however, dimorphic bill size probably helps promote domestic harmony. Larger females do not challenge their mates for hunting locations. Furthermore, males assume the role of principal defenders of nest and territory, liberating the hen to spend more time fattening up for egg production.

Trogon bills are designed to grasp and hold large insects, larvae, small lizards, and slippery berries. In Southeastern Arizona, 11 flycatchers and several other pine-oak woodland species hawk insects in midflight. But their prey items are generally small enough to wholly enclose within the compass of their bills. Like these birds, a trogon is usually airborne when it captures its dinner. Unlike them, the animal food it takes almost always exceeds the dimensions of its bill. To consume a two-inch-long larva, walkingstick, mantis, or katydid, the trogon must fly to a perch and orient its meal longitudinally. The serrations on the upper mandible of a trogon's bill function here like the toothed jaws of a trap to prevent escape.

A second use for the saw-toothed maxillary is to soften hard-bodied food. Often an Elegant Trogon will process a large caterpillar by passing it laterally through its bill one or more times. Once I saw a female pulverize a three-inch-long lizard—typewriter style—for at least five minutes before giving it to a new fledgling. Definitely a case of trogon pablum.

Unlike the decurved bill of birds of prey, the trogon's hook is not used to dice up large portions of meat into edible chunks. Rather, its function is to help secure food items until the bird can perch. Diets of Arizona trogons in the late summer and fall include the fruits of Birchleaf Buckthorn, Southwestern Chokecherry and Canyon Grape. The trogon's hooked bill-tip permits the bird to clamp down and really pull hard—without squirting out the little, ball bearing-like fruits in the process.

V

Trogon Dynamics:
The Sensory Powers

*U*nless I was concealed in a blind, I have never seen a trogon that I felt had not already seen me. Trogons allow themselves to be observed.

If the male is courting the female, showing her prospective nest cavities, he may cavalierly ignore the creak, snap, and crunch of an advancing birdwatcher, or even a group of birdwatchers. Similarly, territorial advertisement, territorial defense, a chokecherry tree drooping with sour purple carps— all may have greater priority for an Elegant Trogon than seeking cover from human eyes.

On the other hand, a calling male trogon can and will move just beyond the periphery of vision in the forest canopy, regardless of how well the wet earth muffles footsteps. And then the bird quietly disappears. I have lost singles, pairs, even family groups in canyons no wider than a fallen pine tree. Too many times.

There is a famous case of Elegant Trogons nesting over a campground fireplace grate in the Chiricahua Mountains, directly in line with the smoke. No evidence suggests they have a sense of smell. Touch is doubtlessly important when they cover their eggs in pitch black cavities, and in food gathering, since their bills are surrounded by stiff, flycatcher-style bristles. But, like most birds, trogons rely primarily upon their eyesight and hearing.

Sight

Canyon walls, which sometimes tower over 3,000 feet above, and a dense, streamside gallery forest create a world of filtered lighting and deep pools of shade in Arizona's premier trogon habitat. On the longest day of the year in South Fork Cave Creek, a trogon nest tree is not apt to receive direct sun till 8:00 a.m.; by 5:00 p.m., the sun has sunk below the western canyon rim. Over 40 percent of a trogon's 15-hour summer day is passed in twilight.

The Elegant Trogon's diet compounds the vision problem—they prefer lethargic, understory insects whose coloration and shape are often designed for camouflage. Because a walking-stick seldom moves, because it likes the jumbled outer crown of low trees and shrubs where twigs terminate, and because its form and color are cryptic, a walkingstick is very difficult for most of its potential enemies to detect. Yet trogons feast on walkingsticks with regularity.

To really appreciate how keen trogon vision is, consider that trogons feed their nestlings about twice as often from 5:00 to 6:00 a.m. as most other hours of the day. At this time in the morning, Whip-poor-wills call in the semiopaque gloom and Coues Whitetail Deer snap limbs as they move ghost-like to their bedding areas. The temperature is still falling and the insects are numb. Under these conditions, a pair of adult trogons will typically catch a half dozen fat, black cicadas for their young in their first hour of activity. Probably, they nail a few for their own breakfasts, as well.

Elegant Trogons also perceive color. Very much like the English Robin, a male trogon pumps up his crimson breast to show strong feelings. These angry red displays are not only meant to attract a mate and to repel other males, they are also intended to show hostility toward intruding jays, squirrels, and even humans.

Obversely, frightened trogons usually perch facing away from the source of danger. To telegraph alarm both sexes lever up their long tails for an instant, then slowly lower them. The signal comes as an abrupt flash of red. Afterwards, the larger outline of the neutral-colored female or the green-backed male tends to dissolve into the landscape.

The ability of the Elegant Trogon to distinguish objects in low intensity light and to discriminate red from other colors relates directly to their eye dynamics. But the importance of vision in the overall ecology of the trogon is exemplified by the flexibility of their neck. A trogon is capable of sweeping its head through an overlapping arc. Like an owl, a trogon can look straight down its spine.

Hearing

The scenario was familiar. Juggling binoculars, pen, and three-by-five inch cards, I would close in on the subject of my study, jotting down notes. Just as I completed the basic background—time, place, number, age, sex, plumage anomalies, vocalizations, and the all-important behavior—along came Joe and Joanne Birdwatcher. Typically, the trogons functioned as my private early warning system, suddenly abdicating perch, feeding station, or prospective nest site for no apparent reason. A minute or two later, my own inferior hearing would pick up the muted conversation and Teabury Shuffle of birdwatchers making forward progress. And I would realize I was wasting my time.

Elegant Trogons can evidently hear each other calling for approximately one-half mile, given a windless day. Under the same conditions, a human being can hear a trogon a quarter mile off. But 0.5 mile is an arbitrary figure that only describes the maximum length of canyon bottom a male is willing to defend in response to other calling males.

It is easily possible that trogons hear territorial advertising at even greater distances and simply elect to avoid conflict. Where trogon density is high in Arizona, in South Fork Cave Creek of the Chiricahua Mountains or Sycamore Canyon in the Atascosas, territories may be spaced much closer. On a crisp May morning in South Fork, three or four cocks may converge at either end of a linear canyon mile. How far they came in response to the sounds of the fracas falls in the realm of pure conjecture.

Hearing plays an absolutely vital role in the life history of the Elegant Trogon. As members of a tropical family of birds which evolved in dense forests, they have had to be conspicuous on an auditory as well as a visual plane. Nonstop vocalizations in the spring and foresummer form a territorial barrier using bricks of sound. Later, the male and his mate duet—exchange antiphonal calls—as a prelude to nest site selection and copulation. Duetting is a pair bonding mechanism shared by other deep forest birds who otherwise might lose contact among the living green curtains.

The need for a quality, interruption-free sound environment continues throughout the trogon breeding cycle. Both sexes take turns at incubation, and nest exchanges are heralded by the calls of the returning bird. After hatching, the young elicit feeding by calling. Whether nestling or fledgling, the parents seem to assume their offspring are sated unless they cry out for food.

The life of an Elegant Trogon is governed by both its ability to hear and to be heard. I have seen courtship stopped cold when a VW microbus sans muffler chugged past a nest hole in South Fork. I have seen nestlings starved while a road grader operated 150 yards away.

It was a typical Fourth of July weekend in 1978 at the U.S. Forest Service campground. Every site was taken and there was stereo music, generators, and fireworks. Later, I found eggshells in the nest there that I had been watching the preceding two weeks. Trogons simply cannot tolerate a polluted sound environment.

VI

Ego

*B*ecause trogons lack exceptional size, speed, or other extra-ordinary defensive mechanisms, they must survive by their courage and wit. They cannot fly very fast or far or resort to group strength for protection.

Their problem is further compounded by a low reproductive rate. Unlike multiple brood species such as Painted Redstarts, or species with large clutches such as Montezuma Quail, Elegant Trogons only nest once per year—and then usually only raise two young. There is no margin for stupidity or cowardice in the trogon's way of life.

Psychology defines the ego as that which organizes thought, governs action, and mediates between instinct and the demands of the environment. It is the only word I know of that bridges the three highest categories of trogon mentality.

Communication

Few birds of the Arizona border ranges are as vocal as the Elegant Trogon. All facets of their life history are presaged by calls that trumpet their moods and which are plainly meant to communicate with other trogons, other animals, and even human beings. Frequently these vocalizations are accompanied by dramatic visual displays.

After years of research, I feel that there are at least eight Elegant Trogon calls that lend themselves to field interpretation:

Koink: This call, used primarily by the male to delimit its territory and to advertise for a female upon its arrival in the spring, is delivered in a series of four to six calls per round, one per second. It almost seems to rhyme with the *oink-oink* ascribed to pigs in nursery tales and has the most metallic quality of any trogon call. Occasionally, the males will tee up in tree tops while *koink*-ing, ignoring human passers-by and displaying their red breasts to full advantage. An unmated male may use this call monotonously all day long, especially if no other males challenge or females answer. If a female does fall under the hypnotic spell of the male's song, she will occasionally respond with a few bars of her own, although only sporadically. Her *koinks* are pitched deeper and sound more hoarse than her mate's, but the distinction is too subtle for most observers to recognize without considerable previous experience with the species.

Koa: Once a territory has been established, either sex may issue a series of *koas* to challenge a trespassing trogon, a flock of Gray-breasted Jays, an Apache Fox Squirrel, or a bird-watcher. But males make use of this call much more than their mates, and frequently they display on a clear perch in full sun as they croak their displeasure in a sequence of three to 50 *koas* in a row. A variation on this same call, *koy,* probably indicates a different level of intensity.

Kow: Paired birds sing this soft and plaintive note antiphonally to maintain contact while foraging in their territory. Males also seem to use this call to coax hens considerable distances up or down canyons to prospective nest trees. In this latter case, it appears to literally mean "come here," although I know it's rank scientific heresy to credit a wild bird with this sort of conscious thought.

Kuh: Low and throaty, this short, monosyllabic note is repeated without interruption until the mood of the trogon changes. Only paired birds use this call and it apparently serves a dual function. First, it shows reproductive interest.

Both sexes utter this note as a prelude to copulation, and the male delivers this call from within the confines of a tree cavity to lure his mate into a prospective nest.

Kuhs are also employed in territorial disputes between two or more males. Often there is considerable chasing and dodging through low, dense vegetation between bouts of vocalizations. Infrequently, the cocks become so aroused that a lengthy sequence of notes leads to a down-spiraling minuet, each male facing the other with its white undertail outspread until they alight on a log or on the bare ground. Here they may perch a foot apart for five minutes or more. Meanwhile, they lean at each other with breasts puffed up, mutter *kuhs*, but refrain from actual contact. Ultimately, the tension proves too great, and one of the combatants flees.

Ha!: This emphatic note is the male's war cry. Seldom heard, it sounds almost like human laughter, but each note of the series is distinct and sharp. Unlike the *Kuh, Ha!* calls are only used by a dominant male as it drives an intruder male out of its territory.

W-k-k: Both sexes use this short, sharp, metallic flight call. It is most apt to come as a trogon explodes off a perch and it may be delivered several times at half second intervals while the bird is airborne. Each rapid utterance lasts approximately half a second. The white undertail rectrices flash fan-like during the flight and reinforce the locational purpose of the vocalization. More often than not, however, Elegant Trogons choose to fly silently.

W-kkkk: Adult trogons use this call to express alarm. Typically, the penetrating opening note trails into a series of hoarse *clucks*. When the bird is extremely agitated, the alarm call accelerates into a rapid, almost unending slur that may continue a minute or longer. This vocalization is invariably accompanied by an upward whip of the tail which reveals the red belly of either sex, before it is slowly lowered. The whole tail pump display only lasts about one second. Trogons use the *W-kkkk* before attacking another species, such as an Apache Fox Squirrel. I have heard female trogons give this shrill call before attacking an intruder female trogon. Use of the alarm indicates either a nest or fledglings are nearby. When birders—knowingly or not—approach too close to either an active nest or young, adult birds always signal their distress with this vocalization.

Interestingly, *W-kkkk* is also the first call in the adult repertoire used by fledglings, generally beginning about a month after they leave the nest. They also accompany the call with the tail pump. When given by fledglings, it seems intended to draw the attention of the parents, to show their location, and to indicate their hunger.

Tu-u: Nestlings and young fledglings deliver an uninterrupted series of clear, evenly spaced, high pitched, bell-like notes that may continue a half hour or longer until they are fed. The *Tu-u* usually seems faintly echoic or quavering, probably because two babies are begging for food simultaneously. When the adults arrive bearing sustenance, they are greeted by an explosive, short-lived chittering that dies away as the babies receive food.

Intelligence

A variety of field experiences impressed me with the ability of *Trogon elegans* to profit from the past. I suspect trogons can remember a successful nest.

Once fledging occurs, the family unit leaves the cavity for the remainder of their stay in Arizona. Then, a minimum of six months later, some trogons apparently manage the salmon-like feat of returning to their home mountain range and even to their nativity canyon. The peg-legged trogon in South Fork used the same quarter mile stretch of canyon bed for three years, for example. But their memory must extend beyond that.

In 1977, I watched a running battle between a first-year male and his probable male parent for the last two weeks of July. The adult bird had already fledged two young before the hatching-year trogon, identified by its heavily barred undertail, even arrived. For two weeks, the cavity in the half-dead oak had been vacant.

Therefore, I was off-guard when, while showing the nest tree to Jim des Lauriers of Chaffee State College, a trogon head suddenly popped out of the hole. Seconds later, the bird caromed off through the sycamore and cypress forest with the adult male in hot pursuit. The two principals re-enacted their primal confrontation on a daily basis for the remainder of the month.

Memory offers the most satisfactory account for the young trogon's behavior—it recognized the cavity it had experienced as a nestling. Since then, I've witnessed other clashes between yearling and adult males over nest chamber proprietorship. One nest in South Fork, first shown to me by des Lauriers, yielded three generations of Elegants before disturbed by a photographer the fourth year. Whether no trogons survive who used the nest, or whether the survivors possibly do remember it, this site has not been occupied since 1977.

Another important Elegant Trogon intelligence trait is their ability to become habituated. A trogon which lives in the Hopkins Fork of Madera Canyon, South Fork Cave Creek, or any other popular locality must adapt to extraordinary birdwatching pressure. As few as a dozen Arizona trogons share the spotlight for tens of thousands of birdwatchers.

Trogons can't and don't ignore the problem; many develop elaborate dodges for fooling the public. But numbers, the birdwatchers' dogged determination, and luck all work against the campground trogon. In a comparatively short time, some bravo males do learn to entertain a certain measure of human attention. At least until they have young in the nest.

Finally—exactly analogous to trapwise mammals, to bears, coyotes, and mountain lions—some trogons become so familiar with tape recorders that they refuse to be baited into view. Here is an indisputable case of reasoning taking precedence over instinct.

Character

Near dawn on July 18, 1978, I found a nest of the Elegant Trogon in Madera Canyon of the Santa Rita Mountains. Only 35 feet away, a family of Cooper's Hawks had set up their own

Immature Cooper's Hawk, attacked by both adult trogons

nursery, and three big, awkward juveniles lunged from tree to tree as they practiced the craft of flight. The adult raptors were nowhere in sight.

As the morning wore on, the periodic hunger cries of the young hawks grew in volume. Meanwhile, the parent trogons came in to feed their nestlings three or four times an hour. Each visit was announced with ringing *Koa's* of challenge; the trogons were clearly disturbed by the noisy antics of their overgrown neighbors.

According to my field notes, the boldest of the fledgling hawks swooped on the male trogon at 9:50 a.m. The male easily dodged. An instant later, the frustrated raptor was attacked by the female trogon, who pecked the back of its head for 10 feet until it could execute an aerial reverse. As the female streaked off, her place was taken by the male trogon. He drove the would-be bird of prey all the way back to its nest tree. Shrill young hawk cries filled the canyon for the next several minutes.

Thus, an introduction to the character of the Elegant Trogon. But the story continues.

Two hours later, the adult female Cooper's Hawk took a perch a short distance up the hillside in the top of a dead snag. The male trogon assumed a perch on a bare oak bough. Whether by design or chance, his chosen position was directly beneath the Cooper's Hawk nest platform. The two birds watched each other in silence for nine minutes.

At 12:06, the female hawk gracefully spread her three-foot-wide wings and sailed down the hill directly over the motionless Elegant. She lit in the enormous Silverleaf Oak that contained the trogon nest cavity. I was trying to write notes when the last act came.

The hawk shot out of the oak so fast the air hissed. She screamed as she struck the trogon's perch. She screamed again as she arced back to her watch post in the snag up the hill. But her talons were empty.

After a moment's search, I found the missing trogon. He was, perhaps, eight feet from his original perch. As I looked on, he began preening, casually rearranging his cool, gray primaries. If he was concerned now about his proximity to either adult or young Cooper's Hawks, it was not evident to me.

The story of the Madera Canyon trogons and their encounter with the Cooper's Hawk family summarizes for me the chief components of trogon dynamics and of trogon ego. Elegant Trogons are capable of swift evasive bursts of flight. They are equipped with keen senses. They are intelligent enough to discriminate between sluggish, inexperienced young hawks and adult raptors who have mastered the art of bird murder.

Most important: they face challenges.

VII

Habitat: How to Find an Elegant Trogon

The Elegant Trogon's chosen habitat in Arizona is Madrean pine-oak woodland. This vegetative association covers over 25 percent of neighboring Mexico, but, in Arizona, pine-oak woodland is sandwiched between desert floor and forested highlands just north of the Sonora line. Here, four small mountain islands—the Atascosa, Santa Rita, Huachuca, and Chiricahua ranges—harbor the entire breeding population found within all the United States.

Moreover, Arizona trogons are confined to major stream corridors that cut through the pine-oak formation. The combination of waters flowing down from the peaks and daily influxes of heat rising off the desert creates a rich, almost tropically luxuriant, gallery forest in the canyon zone where trogons live.

Because Elegant Trogons are canyon dwellers, they are physically protected from many climate extremes. High ridge walls afford shady relief from the Arizona sun and a shield against desiccating summer winds. Canyons promote good cold air drainage. Drought has little effect on the large watersheds since subsurface flow keeps the trees and understory alive and healthy. The double-decker, dense vegetation, in turn, offers yet another buffer of protection against sun, wind, and cold, as well as maintaining a humidity level unusually high for Arizona.

Trogons have, in truth, elected to live in one of the most productive, best protected, and altogether stable environments available to wildlife in all the Southwestern United States. And, as tree cavity nesters, Elegants put an extra inch of insulation between their bodies and the elements.

Patriarchal sycamores identify Arizona's premier trogon canyons. The massive, white trunk of a sycamore may reach 80 feet in height and suspend a canopy of large, star-shaped leaves nearly as wide across. Besides its importance as a host plant for many insects eaten by trogons, it also provides the substrate for two-thirds of all their nests. The soft heartwood of the sycamore is so easily worked by woodpeckers that no other tree supports as many species of borderland hole-nesting birds. Aside from Elegant Trogons, 15 other cavity-dwelling birds also use the Arizona Sycamore.

Like the Elegant Trogon, a number of other neotropical birds are near or at the northern limits of their range in Southeastern Arizona. The list includes the Zone-tailed Hawk, Whiskered Screech-Owl, Sulphur-bellied Flycatcher, Gray-breasted Jay, Montezuma Quail, Strickland's Woodpecker, Mexican Chickadee, Painted Redstart, and the two largest hummingbirds in the U.S.—the Magnificent and the Blue-throated.

All of these species spell potential trogon habitat. The more present, the greater the likelihood that trogons are residents of the avian community as well. But the best indicators are the two carpenters that create nearly all trogon nest cavities.

The Acorn Woodpecker drills holes with entrances approximately 1.6 inches in diameter. Northern Flickers of the red-shafted variety double the entrance size and expand the chamber to trogon dimensions. Fundamental to Acorn Woodpecker ecology is the necessity of snags in which to store acorns, the so-called granary trees. A forestry or fuelwood program that allows the removal of dead or diseased trees subtracts Acorn Woodpeckers. This, in turn, probably reduces the flicker population and the number of nest sites available to medium-sized birds.

Ultimately, the Elegant Trogon population echoes the biotic health of the whole canyon system: living oaks for acorns—

dead trees for acorn granaries—Acorn Woodpeckers to start Northern Flicker nest holes—Northern Flickers to create cavities big enough for small owls, big flycatchers, and the trogon. A good trogon canyon represents good habitat for the whole borderland world of birds.

When I explore an area new to me for Elegant Trogons, I not only look for sycamores, Sierra Madrean birdlife, and woodpecker holes—I listen. Where I hear the serendipity of both Hermit Thrushes and Canyon Wrens, my blood quickens. The habitat *sounds* correct.

The liquid song of the thrush indicates moist conditions, a certain threshold of lush plant growth that fosters abundant insect life. Hermit Thrushes occupy every hectare of the conifer forests in the upper altitudes of Southeastern Arizona. Passing along the Chiricahua Crest Trail in June, a hiker is unendingly bathed in their clear, sweet harmonics. Hermit Thrushes follow the damp fingers of tall timber down the canyon channels to their terminae on the desert's edge at about 5,000 feet elevation. The Arizona-Sonora line marks the approximate southern limit of their breeding range in North America.

Rock and shade control the distribution of Canyon Wrens. The descending series of whistles of the Canyon Wren can be heard throughout the Western deserts, wherever there are cliffs to block light. Their white throat is a special adaptation to a dimly lit environment, flashing on and off as they bob along vertical rock faces, in and out of cracks. It enables families of Canyon Wrens to keep in contact. But, the same cliffs that stop the sun, cut off the heat. Above 6,500 feet in most Arizona locations, the bare stone walls are too cold and sterile to permit much wren food to exist.

There is a blend zone where the habitat requirements of both Hermit Thrush and Canyon Wren overlap. Here, conditions are moist, shady, hot. Streamside forest hinges against a vertical plane of stone. To me, a Southeastern Arizona dawn counterpunctuated with the clarinet-like melody of the Hermit Thrush and the bright, descending cadences of the Canyon Wren, offers the promise of an Elegant Trogon as nothing else can.

Cathedral Rock, 700 feet high, dominates Cave Creek Canyon
of the Chiricahua Mountains

VIII

Population and Distribution: Nucleus Canyons

*I*n May, 1977, I pitched my nylon backpacker tent in South Fork Cave Creek of the Chiricahua Mountains. After I finished, I sat down and wrote the first entry in my journal: "Doubts about everything." Then—right on cue—a male Elegant Trogon flew into my camp and issued a series of challenge calls. I have been counting trogons ever since.

Finally, I think I have a clear picture of trogon population and distribution. Each of the four border ranges where Elegants are known to breed contains at least one major canyon with exceptional biological diversity. Here, under sheltering walls, a diamond strand of water wells to the surface at intermittent points, in and out of drought. Along its course, virtually every plant and animal native to that particular mountain is able to find a niche.

I think of these watersheds as the "nucleus" canyons of the Atascosa, Santa Rita, Huachuca, and Chiricahua Mountains. Like a cell nucleus, each canyon packages the biological wealth of the entire range into a small area. The Rocky Mountain birds are here, as well as the Sierra Madrean; and here, too, almost all species achieve their highest population.

The four nucleus trogon canyons in the United States are Sycamore Canyon in the Atascosa Mountains, Madera Canyon in the Santa Rita Mountains, Sunnyside Canyon in the Huachuca Mountains, and the Cave Creek system in the Chiricahua Mountains. Of the 100 or so adult Elegant Trogons in Southeastern Arizona, approximately half live in the nucleus canyons.

The Atascosa Mountains

Atasco is Spanish for an obstruction to passage. Back in 1854, a member of the U.S. Boundary Survey, mapping newly acquired Gadsden Purchase lands, described this range as an "upheaved, boiling volcanic pool." His description of the landmass was so accurate that today these mountains are arbitrarily divided into four groups: the Tumacacoris, Mule Ridge, Pajaritos (a Spanish word meaning little bird), and the Atascosas.

One canyon—Sycamore—siphons the heart of the area. Its headwaters drain 6,440-foot-high Atascosa Peak, and its outlet emerges on the Mexican border at an elevation of 3,500 feet. Mexican Pinyon Pine, Silverleaf Oak, and New Mexican Locust grow at lower elevations in Sycamore Canyon than any other U.S. location.

Sycamore Canyon is one of the United States' most prized natural history museums. In 1970, 545 acres in upper Sycamore were officially withdrawn from grazing when the canyon was designated as the Goodding Research Natural Area by the Chief of the Forest Service. Today, the entire length of the canyon is closed to overnight camping without a special permit, and the use of fires is prohibited.

Leslie N. Goodding, a prominent Arizona botanist, first drew national attention to the area's unique floral community in 1946 with the publication of an article titled "A Hidden Botanical Garden." Fourteen type specimens of plants have been collected in the United States from Sycamore Canyon, including a species of ash tree named for Goodding. More widespread forms include *Asplenium exiguum*, a fern that also grows in the Himalayan Mountains, and a member of the tropical bromeliad family, Tillandsia recurvata. One-seed Juniper is the most important host for showy arrays of the tillandsia, an off-white air plant that clings to limbs and resembles a sea urchin. Junipers festooned with tillandsia begin to appear below the Upper Box, about one mile down canyon from the Hank and Yank Spring parking area.

The pronounced Mexican influence on the vegetation found in Sycamore is mirrored in its wildlife. Sonoran Chub, a small fish otherwise limited to the Rio de la Concepción watershed below the border, has managed to survive here through both drought and flash flood. So had—at least through 1980— the Tarahumara Frog, endemic to the Sierra Madre Occidental, elsewhere unknown in the United States.

However, while the disjunct ranges of this fish and amphibian probably date back to a wetter period in Sonoran regional history, the duration that Sycamore has harbored Rose-throated Becards and Five-striped Sparrows is much less certain. Bill Harrison, a biology teacher from Nogales, alertly noted the presence of the becards here in 1974. Three years later, Harrison again was the first to detect Five-striped Sparrows.

Elegant Trogons apparently colonized Sycamore Canyon early in 1975, when government botanist Jack Kaiser discovered a pair near the Penasco tributary. Kaiser had collected flora in Sycamore starting in 1941, but April 17, 34 years later, marked his first trogon sighting. Since then, trogons have flourished in the five miles of extremely rugged, trailless canyon below Hank and Yank Spring. I have never found fewer than four males; on a June visit in 1979, I saw six separate cocks defending territories. These birds are concentrated in the same zone as the tillandsia. Where pine-oak woodland yields to hillsides dominated by Giant Sahuaro cactus, approximately one mile north of the Mexican border, Elegant Trogons give way to Five-striped Sparrows.

Water—its presence or absence—guards the Sycamore Canyon population of Elegants with exaggerated jealousy. Summer temperatures often exceed 100 degrees Fahrenheit, and the reflector-oven effect of spectacular cliffs transforms the stretches of sluggish water into a bright green soup seasoned with insect corpses. At the other extreme, flash floods have written the story of their passage 12 feet above the canyon floor. Flash floods can occur at any time of the year in Sycamore Canyon.

The Santa Rita Mountains

Writing for a natural history journal in 1936, A. J. van Rossem summarized his experiences in Madera Canyon with these words: "Regardless of its status in former years, this trogon may now be counted a fairly common summer visitant in the Santa Ritas." But Madera Elegant Trogons suffered hard times over the next two decades.

Aside from direct attrition caused by illegal specimen collection, the road up Madera was improved, cabins were constructed, and campgrounds were modernized. Van Rossem reports finding a gunshot female near a campground in 1931—left to rot. After the discovery of the first U.S. trogon nest by Arthur A. Allen, Madera became a national attraction. After the end of World War II, a new wave of Arizonans discovered the shady camping and picnicking facilities under Madera's big oaks and sycamores.

Tucson birdwatchers and conservationists Ross and Florence Thornberg concluded that only one pair of Elegant Trogons used Madera Canyon in 1948, none at all in 1949. Joe T. Marshall, Jr., in his classic 1957 monograph, *Birds of Pine-Oak Woodland in Arizona and Adjacent Mexico,* simply lists the trogon as "reported" from the Santa Rita Mountains.

Free enterprise, in all probability, reached the Santa Ritas long before *Trogon elegans.*

Jesuit priests established Arizona's first gold and silver mines at the base of the peaks in the late 1600s; Arizona's first sawmill was situated in Madera Canyon in 1857. Madera actually means lumber in Spanish. Soon after, the two highest summits in the range, Mount Hopkins and Mount Wrightson, acquired their names in memory of two pioneer miners killed in the mid-1860s by Apache Indians. Mount Wrightson is also unofficially known as "Old Baldy"—not only because the top is a bare granite dome, but reputedly to honor Richard S. Ewell, a frontier Army captain.

Seen from west or east, the Santa Ritas are a 15-mile-long crescent of blue capped with cold, jagged granite. At 9,453 feet, Mount Wrightson towers over a mile above the surrounding desert. Three miles away, separated by 7,100-foot Josephine Saddle, Mount Hopkins swells to 8,585 feet in elevation and provides a home for an observatory operated by the Smithsonian Institute. Madera Canyon plumbs both major summits of the Santa Rita Mountains.

The drainage is shaped like a colossal crow's foot. Three tributaries, one each from Mount Wrightson, Josephine Saddle, and Mount Hopkins, join the main stem well over 3,000 feet below the peaks. Each fork contains permanent springs, stringers of sycamore, and giant specimens of Silverleaf Oak. Each also contains Elegant Trogons.

The history of modern trogon research really begins in Madera Canyon with Edward Steele of Tucson, a businessman who devoted many of his early mornings to unknotting problems of the trogon's life history in the shade of Mount Wrightson. Working throughout the 1960s, Steele estimated the Elegant population in Madera at one or two pairs.

My own census results show the total number has since more than doubled. Since 1978, Madera has typically had eight to 12 adult trogons. Over 40 years earlier, van Rossem, too, reported eight trogons from Madera Canyon. But, as history reveals, the population of Elegant Trogons in Madera Canyon is a treasure easily lost through man's thoughtlessness.

The Huachuca Mountains

Lying astride the U.S. frontier with Sonora, Mexico, the Huachuca Mountains rise on the Arizona side in a 20-mile series of summits ranging between 8,410 and 9,466 feet in elevation. Long strands of evergreen oak savannah connect the Huachucas with other mountain groups below the international boundary. It was here that the last Mexican Wolves to breed in Arizona were exterminated in 1942, when a male and six cubs were clubbed to death by a federal trapper. And it was here that Arizona's first Elegant Trogon was collected in 1885. Arbitrary political lines have had less ecological importance for the Huachuca range than the simple facts of biogeography.

In 1979, I organized the first "Huachuca Mountain Trogon Day Census" with the help of the late John Epler, president of the Huachuca Audubon Society. The following account is taken from the society's *Trogon News:*

> Twenty-four members of the Huachuca Audubon Society arose before dawn this past June 23 and quietly entered the canyons of the Huachuca Mountains. Their purpose was to completely census all of the Elegant Trogon habitat in the area in a single day. The results were spectacular: 28 adult trogons were recorded in 42 miles of canyon bottom land. Of the 20 canyons and tributaries surveyed, 12 harbored Arizona's most sought-after bird.
>
> An added bonus to the census results were three nests discovered by Doug Danforth; Ted Miller, Bob and Katie Crooks; and myself. The Miller-Crooks nest was the first ever recorded in a man-made substrate—an abandoned utility pole modified for occupancy by woodpeckers. Furthermore, the Huachuca Mountains produced a canyon complex, Sunnyside-Scotia, that yielded 13 adult trogons alone.

By 4:00 a.m. on June 23, eggs were frying in the skillet at our camp on the remote southwestern slope of the Huachuca Mountains. Bettina Martin and I drank our hot coffee by lantern light as we talked over census routes. Bettina, a summer volunteer at the American Museum of Natural History's Southwestern Research Station, had been assigned Scotia Canyon; I was taking Sunnyside. Gradually the black silhouettes of Chihuahua Pine on the divide separating the two canyons became sharp. The calls of the Whiskered Screech Owl gave way to the "Jose Maria" of a Greater Pewee. It was time to enter the canyons.

> These excerpts are from my field notes for the morning:
>
> 4:50—Cool, about 55-60 degrees. Still. Clear. Creek barely running.
>
> 5:57—Male trogon calling. Eureka Canyon tributary is running a trickle. Second trogon, probable female, joins first bird. Huachuca Gray Squirrel is in flicker hole in White Oak here.
>
> 6:35—Painted Redstart nest with young just above Mud Spring.

6:52—First direct sun in canyon bottom, but only touches isolated places. Mainly shadow.

7:00—Band-tailed Pigeon.

7:35—*Nest!* Found trogon nest about 12 feet up in living Silverleaf Oak about 100 feet from where I had Sunnyside nest last year. Male was brooding young when I arrived. Did not flush until I was five feet from nest tree. Used *Koa* call.

8:29—Trogon 100 feet inside major east tributary of Sunnyside. Male.

9:55—Two male trogons in White Pine about 0.75 mile up East Fork. *Kuh*'ed. At each other, I think, not me. One male caught larva 20-25 feet in White Pine. One male has splotchy red breast.

10:30—Topped out on purple rock conglomerate with small seep in upper end of Sunnyside. Elevation 7,500 feet. Mucho Gambel Oak and Douglas Fir. Red-faced Warblers numerous here.

I got back to camp in midafternoon. My tally for the day was six male and three female Elegant Trogons. Over cold refreshments from the ice chest, Bettina told me she had two pairs in Scotia.

The Chiricahua Mountains

The Cave Creek Canyon complex on the eastern massif of the Chiricahua Mountains holds more Elegant Trogons than any other drainage in Arizona. Shaped like a giant letter "Y" and cut 3,000 feet into the red rhyolite crust of the range, main Cave Creek and its major tributary, South Fork, reach all the way back to the 9,700-foot crest of Southern Arizona's biggest mountain.

The Chiricahuas are the only border range to span five of North America's seven life zones. Highest in elevation is the Hudsonian Life Zone; the southernmost Engelmann Spruce in the United States shade Cave Creek's headwaters above 9,000 feet. Layered below, depending on altitude and exposure, are: the Canadian Life Zone, indicated by Douglas Fir and aspen stands; the Ponderosa Pines of the Transition Life Zone; a rich infusion of Mexican oaks and Madrean pines in the Upper

Sonoran Life Zone; and—at Cave Creek's 4,700-foot outlet—the White-thorn Acacia, Mesquite, and Creosote of the desert, or Lower Sonoran Life Zone.

Only the Arctic-alpine and Tropical environments are absent altogether from Cave Creek Canyon.

Life zones and the vertical stature of the range probably exert no more influence on the Chiricahua plant and animal community than its geographic position. The mountain sits at the axis of one U.S. and three great Mexican biological provinces. The Rocky Mountains, the Sierra Madres, the Chihuahuan Desert, and the Sonoran Desert all contribute flora and fauna unique to their region. In the Chiricahuas, Broad-tailed, Blue-throated, Lucifer, and Anna's Hummingbirds, each representative of a different geographical region, may all compete for space at one flowering Cave Creek agave.

And a final ecological factor: the Chiricahuas are large. Extending 40 miles north-south by 20 miles in width, the Huachuca, Santa Rita, and Atascosa Mountains would all fit inside the perimeter of the massive Chiricahuas. Trees like Engelmann Spruce and Arizona Cypress, as well as mammals like the Cliff Chipmunk and the Apache Fox Squirrel have managed to survive the past 8,000 years of drying conditions on this mountain island, while other populations have died out in the smaller border ranges. In the language of the Apache Indian, Chiricahua means "big mountain."

Main Cave Creek has been inhabited by European man for over a century. The log cabin homesteader Stephen Reed built in 1879 now rests on property owned by the Southwestern Research Station of the American Museum of Natural History. And the main stem drainage has seen some changes, too. Grazing has fostered thickets of Catclaw Acacia; fuelwood and timber harvest, in conjunction with fire control, has encouraged Alligator Juniper invasion; and agriculture has introduced apple trees and alfalfa.

Most of my Elegant Trogon research has been conducted in the South Fork, a 10-mile-long arm of the Cave Creek watershed. Nowhere else is the rich biotic diversity of Southeastern Arizona better expressed. And nowhere else in all of Arizona has man permitted a canyon that razors through five life zones to go commercially unexploited. South Fork has never been mined, logged, tilled, overgrazed, or dammed. The vine-strung, pastel ribbon of trees that ties the desert Ocotillos to the conifer forest in South Fork is, in a sense, the last living picture of the original ecology of the borderland ranges. It is a picture that is still evolving.

On October 23, 1977, I had the privilege of reporting the first Eared Trogon ever found north of Sonora from the South Fork of Cave Creek. The hefty, 13-inch-long trogon was feasting on a spectacular fall crop of Arizona Madrone berries. Before the season ended, three more of these handsome red, green, and blue-tailed birds joined the first in South Fork Canyon.

The Eared Trogon is the rarest member of the family *Trogonidae* in North America. Although lacking their splashy, three-foot-long tail coverts, Eared Trogons are the closest in size and the nearest relative to the Resplendent Quetzals of the Middle American cloud forest. Sightings almost every year since tend to support my hypothesis that somewhere in the rugged vastness of upper South Fork there must be at least one pair of breeding Eared Trogons.

Six to 10 pairs of Elegant Trogons nest annually in South Fork. Twice now, I have seen the smaller Elegant attack his big, Madrean highland relative in this wilderness preserve. The explosive clash of sound and color of those encounters, set in virgin forest under immense, volcanic cliffs, justifies, for me, South Fork Cave Creek's reputation as the trogon capitol of the United States.

IX

The Yearly Round

Arrival

*F*or eight years, the initiation of a new season's trogon research quickened my blood every April. True, one and sometimes several Elegants overwinter almost annually, but for me, the year only began when the first arriving cocks sounded their impassioned challenges to all comers. Ordinarily, the month of April marked the onset of the trogon breeding cycle.

Members of the Chiricahua Apache Indian tribe divide the year into six parts. In April, the last frosts of "Little Eagles" gradually relax their grip on the northern outliers of the Sierra Madre and a new season begins they call "Many Leaves." The most conspicuous leaves in the canyons I surveyed from 1977 to 1984 belonged to Arizona Sycamores. This transformation from bare, boyish trunks and limbs to girlish trees ornamented with newly emergent, star-shaped foliage is largely accomplished in the month of April.

April also signals the beginning of the dry season. For 90 to 100 days each year, all rains practically cease, and desiccating winds sweep down the broad desert valleys of the region. Not so in the mountain canyons. Protected by cliffs and blessed with water—icy snow melt from the headwaters above—the streamside gallery forest sends out a million green shoots to greet the lengthening day. Paradoxically, a kind of autumn ushers in this change.

The oaks of the border ranges are spring deciduous. Derived from parent stock in the Sierra Madre, they drop their dull red and yellow leaves in late March and early April as an adaptation to conserve water during the dry months. With built-in metabolic wisdom, however, they releaf immediately if there is sufficient ground moisture. And there is in the deep soils of the riparian corridors where trogons dwell.

In contrast to the cloth-like, olive-green foliage of the sycamores, the oaks produce leaves as bright and crisp as celery tops. Canyon bottoms change into multihued ribbons of garden green. At this tender stage, Silverleaf, Netleaf, Emory, and Arizona White Oak provide a nutrient-rich salad for millions of herbivorous larvae. The first Elegant Trogons time their arrival to capitalize on this April explosion of arthropods.

But they do not arrive as a wave. While almost any still, moonlit night in April may introduce a new male or a pair of trogons to South Fork in the Chiricahuas or Madera Canyon in the Santa Ritas, most nights bring none. Population recruitment proceeds at a crawl. The full complement of *Trogon elegans* is not in place until the end of June.

Alexander Skutch speculated that pairs of the closely related Mountain Trogon he watched in Guatemala shared the same territory and "maintain some loose association" during the winter months. Elegant Trogons often seem to arrive in the border ranges already paired. In Arizona, I never observed a female that was long without a male. The sex ratio in all the mountains taken together averaged about two males for every female. In South Fork and Cave Creek in the Chiricahuas, which always harbor the largest concentration of trogons in the U.S., there is only a surplus of two or three males.

Whether mated or not, the voices of male Elegant Trogons fill the principal borderland canyons in April and May.

Territory

The average length of a territory in the trogon canyons of Arizona is about one-half mile. In favorable situations such as Sycamore Canyon in the Atascosas or South Fork in the

Chiricahuas, territories can be crowded three to a mile. I once found two trogon nests only 200 yards apart in South Fork Cave Creek. But, in the small canyons on the hot, south face of the Huachucas, a single resident pair will advertise a territory a full mile in length.

All through the long foresummer, arriving cock trogons try to whittle down existing territories and elope with resident females should any be present. Frequently these late arrivals are males hatched the preceding year, readily aged by remnant teardrops behind the eyes, heavily barred undertails like an adult female, and pinkish-orange breasts and bellies. Nonetheless, the yearling males do occasionally carve out a territory and win a mate.

If an unmated female intrudes upon an occupied territory, the resident hen assumes the responsibility of driving her off. Unlike their male siblings, no plumage traits give away a female's age. I often wondered if these roving birds were not progeny from the preceding year's nest, returning to their home territory. If so, they received no quarter from their parents.

The common denominator every trogon territory must possess is a significant tributary. Tall trees with a well-developed stratum of understory ordinarily mark the junction of a side canyon. Nearly half of the 50-odd nests I recorded were located exactly at the confluence, and the median distance away was only 150 feet. Clearly the confluence groves are also the same groves females prefer for their nests.

Luxuriant plant growth offers the pairs an abundant food supply, dense cover for escaping swift-flying hawks, and usually a good selection of potential nest cavities. Nests of Elegant Trogons in Arizona have an average of 10 species of trees within a 100-foot radius, the richest tree diversity of any woodland or forest habitat in the Southwest. By far, the most important two species were Arizona White Oak and Arizona Sycamore.

Arizona White Oak is the preferred substrate for well over one-third of all trogon feeding attempts. The denizens of white oak canopy foliage, first lepidopteran larvae, then cicadas, and finally orthopterans, katydids and walkingsticks, furnish Elegants with a changing assortment of proteins as the year progresses.

Sycamore is important not only because it is the tree selected for two-thirds of all Arizona trogon nests. Mature sycamores typically harbor enough woodpecker cavities for every member of the pine-oak hole-nesting community of birds. Canyons without sycamore rarely host breeding Elegant Trogons.

The premier territories also have surface water. A stretch of living stream or a pothole spring encourages plant growth, fruit production, and large populations of edible arthropods. Sycamores are almost entirely confined to canyons with permanent water. Several times I've had the pleasure of watching trogons bathe.

As inglorious as children, the birds plop into pools from perches a few feet high, thrash furiously for a couple of feet, dunk heads and totally immerse their bodies, and then explode out of the water to a nearby perch. A good perch may be used several times in succession. Bathing may be solitary or enjoyed with a sibling.

The scarcity of water in the boundary mountains of Arizona probably accounts for the number of territories that split on the axis of a spring. But water isn't an absolute perquisite for a trogon territory. In the drought year of 1981, only a single seep persisted the entire 4.5-mile length of Sunnyside Canyon in the Huachucas. The total number of trogons in Sunnyside actually increased from 1980 to 1981.

Courtship

One April day, I watched a male show a female four different nest sites. Courtship consists of the male leading a female up or down the drainage to a possible nursery chamber, persistently calling *Kow* all the while. This may take hours while she coyly forages on practically every intervening oak in the whole canyon. Perhaps she is simply assessing the resource base upon which she must raise a couple of ravenous offspring.

Usually the cock arrives at the hole well ahead of the female and clings to the lower edge of its entrance like a woodpecker, bracing itself with its tail. When she draws near, he enters the cavity headfirst and utters soft *Kuhs* from within. With luck and patience, she will join him. They may stay quietly inside the nest hole for the next half hour. Considering the average dimensions of these chambers, it's almost impossible to imagine how two grown trogons can find the room.

The male is the first to reemerge. Somehow it turns a somersault, squeezes past the hen and flies to a nearby perch. Possibly there are aspects of the cavity that she needs to reflect upon alone. After a hiatus of several minutes—or longer—she rejoins the male. Ultimately, exchanging *Kuh* notes, soft yet intense, they copulate. Copulation seems to occur no less than once a day throughout courtship and continues, at least sporadically, until the young leave the nest.

The female often rejects the first few holes shown to her by her mate. She may or may not even enter a prospective nest. The process may take several days or even weeks. Two months after I saw the male show his mate the four nest holes, I found him brooding young in the fourth and final one. Working back in time, no less than a full month elapsed before she accepted the nest and laid her eggs.

The Nest

Just a half mile above the parking area in Madera Canyon, a pair of Elegant Trogons nested four consecutive years in a sycamore only 75 feet off the main trail, plainly visible to literally thousands of delighted birdwatchers. The cavity was 43 inches deep. No other trogon nest I ever measured even approached this, but—especially because it was frequently disturbed—I believe it does exemplify the premium Elegant Trogons place on depth. The average sycamore cavity nest is some 19 inches deep, oak and pine nests are less than 12. Sycamore cavities are selected two to one over other tree substrates.

Woodpeckers create nearly all trogon nest holes. Both the average and the median long dimension of the nest opening is four inches, better than twice the size of Acorn Woodpecker entrances, and both the average and median measurement for the nest interior is 5½ inches, half again larger than those for Acorns. Obviously the author of these nests is the Red-shafted race of the Northern Flicker, the largest woodpecker in Arizona.

I spent years trying to develop my search image for trogon nests. As a consequence I can tell you there are literally *thousands* of woodpecker holes in the riparian forests of Arizona's boundary mountains. Sometimes I felt like my routes—say Hank and Yank Spring in Sycamore Canyon five miles down to the Mexican line—were merely connect-the-dot games conducted on a grotesque scale.

But, over the years, I did finally develop a certain proficiency at predicting which "dots" would harbor active nests.

After a decided preference for sycamore, the overall condition of the tree is the most significant clue. Elegants use dead or dying trees almost twice as often as living wood. Even in healthy trees, nests are often located at the juncture of a dead branch with the main trunk.

Part of my job was to climb the tree and measure every ramification of the cavity. Trogons nest an average of 25½ feet above the ground. Most nests are situated in the upper third of the tree. Once I measured a sycamore hole in Cave Creek of the Chiricahua Mountains that was 48 feet 10 inches high. Invariably, tiny ants had a thriving colony somewhere up the trunk and seemingly infiltrated my sweat-soaked T-shirts without even trying. The lowest nest I ever recorded was only 8 feet 1½ inches up a Silverleaf Oak in Sunnyside Canyon of the Huachuca Mountains. I could drive right up to the nest tree. I'll never forget the tremendous satisfaction I got from sitting on top the cab of my pickup documenting the *least* impressive nest of an Elegant Trogon I ever found.

Considerable competition exists among midsized cavity dwellers for flicker cavities. I have watched male Elegant Trogons battle female flickers for hours. Trogons usurp the flickers' nest during the fray, but ultimately the flickers win the cavity. Whiskered Screech-Owls, another pine-oak woodland specialty bird in southeastern Arizona, are also dominant over Elegants. Twice in successive years in Sunnyside Canyon in the

Huachuca Mountains I saw Whiskereds take possession of former trogon nests before the trogons returned to claim them. Whiskered Screech-Owls ultimately wound up acquiring about 10 percent of all the trogon nests for which I had a history.

In 1981, Burdette White watched the most protracted and ferocious nest site struggle on record. In the course of that breeding season, a pair of Sulphur-bellied Flycatchers attacked a pair of Elegant Trogons over 200 different times, even knocking their feathers off in the skirmishes. Burdette believed the Sulphur-bellies were simply trying to reclaim a nest they used in 1980. The 1981 trogon pair not only sustained the Sulphur-belly onslaught, they successfully fledged three young.

Their nest was located in a sycamore on the lower end of Stewart Campground in the Chiricahua Mountains. Trogons also occupied the site two years earlier in 1979. This devotion to a specific nest cavity plays an important role in the ecology of the Elegant Trogon. Better than a quarter of the nest trees I detected in the course of my field work were reused, although not necessarily in successive years. More impressive was that because some sites were occupied three or more years, almost a full 50 percent of all Elegant Trogon nestings were in known nest cavities. Apparently indifferent to the prospect of renewed onslaughts by Sulphur-bellied Flycatchers, the Stewart Campground nest was readopted by trogons once again in 1982.

Eggs

By the first week of May, while perhaps half of the trogon population has yet to arrive, some pairs are already caring for eggs. In June, the number of incubating birds reaches its maximum. Two oval white eggs complete the standard clutch, but three eggs are not uncommon and three times I recorded nests containing four eggs. Far down in Sycamore Canyon in the Atascosa Mountains, only a mile or so from the Mexican border, I once found a male bird incubating a single egg.

Oddly, on May 23, 1982, a female trogon being watched by birders in Cave Creek, abruptly flew down to the ground and laid an egg. It measured 30 by 24 millimeters.

Two years later, I had the opportunity to measure an entire clutch without disturbing the nest. A week of heavy rains had forced a pair to abandon a cavity that opened to sky. Four dingy white eggs were floating in several inches of water at the bottom. I asked my son to fish them out. The eggs were 32 to 33 millimeters in length by 22 to 23 millimeters in width— slightly over an inch long by about three-quarters-inch wide. All four contained embryos. This was the only case I ever encountered of a pair of trogons attempting to renest after the original nest failed.

Trogons are extremely nest attentive, occupying the nest from 85 to 95 percent of the day. Each sex takes two turns of incubation each day. The hen, who covers the eggs overnight, is usually relieved by the male between 5:00 and 6:00 a.m.

Many groggy-eyed birders in Cave Creek and Madera Canyon have been treated to a sight and sound show before daybreak as a cock brazenly flew through their campground, trumpeting challenges en route to its nest. Once ensconced on the eggs, however, the male surrenders responsibility for defending their territory to its mate. A female will attack any interloping females, males, or even pairs of Elegants for the next couple of hours. As a rule, no matter how pitched or near the confrontation, the male sits tight until relieved. After a 1½- to 2½-hour long session, there is another nest exchange. Uttering soft *Kows*, the male exits and the female enters without further ceremony.

All is quiet at the nest tree for a variable length of time that the female seems to control. Some hens leave the nest again an hour or so later, some hold fast till one o'clock in the afternoon. Regardless of the duration of her second session, the male is usually there to replace her.

This is the heat of the day in the border canyons. Temperatures may hover around 90 degrees Fahrenheit, humidities are over 50 percent, and the cavities are suffocating. Males put in a two- to four-hour stint during the afternoon. Toward the end, they may come to the entrance and call plaintively, but the female does not respond. Males incubating in June often gape at the entrance for half an hour, obviously in distress from the heat, bills open to full compass, using a gular flutter to cool down. But only when the sun wanes between late afternoon and dusk does the male finally desert the nest. Even then he may return once or twice to inspect the eggs, but usually no further incubation takes place.

The eggs remain unattended until the hen returns to the nest to roost. During June, Venus may be well above the craggy canyon rim before the female slips into the cavity, sometimes as late as 7:30 p.m.

Hatching comes 22 or 23 days after the first egg is laid. Assuming a one-day interval between egg-laying sessions at the onset, actual full-time incubation is probably 17 or 18 days. At most nests, the eggs hatch in late June or July. In the Apache calendar, it is now the season known as "Large Leaves."

Nestlings

I will never forget the smell of the predawn air as I hurried up a wet trail to reach a blind before the trogons awakened. The damp canyons were alive with scents that ranged from moldy wood to wild rose, from citrus-rank Hoptree to vanilla-sweet Chihuahua Pine. "Large Leaves" signals the onset of the summer rainy season in the boundary mountains of southeastern Arizona. A pattern develops in late June as the storm track settles into place. Afternoon or evening showers commence about the same time every day, come every day for a week, then withdraw below the border a few days or even a week, gathering strength for a renewed assault.

On most rainy days, the morning breaks cloud free, but tumid with humidity. By 10:00 a.m., big, white cumulus clouds boil up over the peaks, and, by noon, the first rumbles of thunder glance off the cliffs and roll down the canyons. The sky above oscillates from liquid blue to lead gray. Some days, by 3:00 p.m. (some summers not till 5:00 or 7:00), the first big drops splash down and presage the deluge to come. I would listen to the reassuring drum on the tarp roof of my blind, imagining the baby trogons huddled in their nest, and feel that all was well in the world.

Both parents brood the young after hatching, and some brooding continues throughout the first week. The female spends slightly more time in the nest than the male. At this stage, the nestlings are entirely unfeathered and their eyes are glued shut. Even after the hen stops brooding during the daytime, she continues to roost in the cavity at night until the young are about 12 days old. By now, the nestlings are largely covered in their natal down, with the exception of bare lower abdomens, and only the primaries and the rectrices have yet to burst free from horny black sheaths.

As the young enter their second week, both adults accelerate the number of feeding visits each makes to the nest each day. Between 5:00 and 6:00 a.m. is the most important hour. The young are fed an average of five times before the sun soars above the canyon walls. The next hour, they are fed four times. Altogether the parents will pay the nest between 40 and 50 feeding visits in the 15 hours between 5:00 a.m. and 8:00 p.m. Insects constitute almost all the food the young trogons receive for their first two weeks.

A tremendous rasping noise—shrill as a skill saw—pulses through the canyons in late June and early July. It is the fevered cacophony of male cicadas vibrating their abdominal plates to attract mates. I remember once finding an Arizona Cypress trunk in the South Fork of the Chiricahuas festooned with hundreds of translucent nymph cases. Amber and empty, their perfect little chitinous exoskeletons gave eery testimony to the great slumbering life that had concealed itself underground for years. Some unknown impulse had sent every individual of the myriad organism swarming up the trunk of the mighty cypress on a single night.

In a remarkable chrysalis, their clear wings emerge before dawn. After mating, the females lay their eggs in twig stems, the injured twigs fall to earth, and the young cicadas begin their subterranean existence. Within a few weeks or a month, the adults die without having ever eaten.

Every summer, a new cicada hatch provides a reliable staple in the diet of the trogon chicks. Both parents have an equal share in feeding their young. For the two months cicadas are available, the adult trogons seem capable of catching them at will, even on the coldest morning before the first glow of sunrise. Aside from numerous cicadas, the adults bring their offspring moths, butterflies, katydids, and walkingsticks. In their third week in the nest, they may even treat the young to a small, well-pulverized Mountain Spiny Lizard.

Since 14 days old, the young Elegants have been scaling the nest walls and receiving food at the entrance. In between feedings, the mellow tooting of their voices, similar to the call of a Northern Pygmy-Owl, may continue monotonously for hours in the late afternoon. Although the young are born with papillate heel pads that protect them from the unlined wooden floor of the nest chamber, nothing elevates them above the accumulating debris of their own excreta, undigested foot parts, and even the egg shells from which they hatched. Yet they remain clean, apparently unaffected by a thriving colony of ectoparasites swarming through their newly emerging plumage.

As the nestlings complete their third week of life, the adults introduce fruit into their diet. The pea-sized berries of Birchleaf Buckthorn turn bright red in midsummer, just as the young trogons begin to teeter experimentally at the nest orifice. But the adults seem increasingly reluctant to feed their offspring anything at all. Instead, one or the other parent bird perches minutes at a time, 10 or 15 feet from the entrance, clearly withholding a scarlet buckthorn berry or a succulent green katydid. While the young beg with incessant, echoic *Tu-u* notes, the adult merely shifts the burden in its bill. It may even fly off still clutching the unused food item. Or it may eat it. Now only hours remain till the young attempt their maiden flight.

Not all nests will succeed. Causes of failure vary from drowning to nest abandonment owing to human photographic activities. I saw Cooper's Hawks attack the parent trogons on several occasions and I saw parent trogons attack Apache Fox Squirrels in the Chiricahuas and Arizona Gray Squirrels in the Huachuca and Santa Rita Mountains. Wendy Hakes, conducting a trogon nest box program in Ramsey Canyon, observed both Ringtails and Coati investigating her artificial cavities. Only half of the nests I watched in South Fork and Cave Creek ultimately produced young.

Fledglings

Between 20 and 23 days of age—if all goes well—the first fledgling commits itself to the realm of the air. Twenty feet seems to be about the limit for a young Elegant. Still lacking much of a tail and having never exercised its wings, it flutters furiously in a descending curve that ends abruptly when it runs into a shrub or crashes to earth. The first fledging I ever saw took place on July 9, 1979. In six hours, the young trogon flew 446 feet and used 14 perches. Three of these were on the ground.

At another nest on July 30, two fledglings completed their day within 100 feet of their natal cavity. One bird roosted 15 feet high in an Arizona Cypress. The other found a perch about eight feet above the ground in a Silverleaf Oak. The young settled down about 50 feet apart. Each fledgling was attended exclusively by one parent trogon.

A third chick remained in the nest, either less mature or less experimental than its cohorts. I returned an hour before dawn to learn the fate of the last nestling. Even before the Whip-poor-wills stopped calling, the little trogon began to vocalize. It piped its quavering *Tu-u* nonstop without attracting either adult for four hours. Desperate, it launched itself from the nest at 9:00 a.m. In just 40 minutes, resting only seven times, it covered 200 feet. When the adult male finally fed it at 9:40 a.m., the intrepid youngster had fasted at least 18 hours.

New trogon fledglings are particularly vulnerable to predation. The July 9 fledgling was attacked its first morning out of the nest by a flock of Gray-breasted Jays. One of the July 30 chicks was attacked by a Sulphur-bellied Flycatcher.

Both times it was the female parent that came to the defense of her young. Both times she had no recourse but to cover the body of her offspring by shielding it with one outspread wing. Possibly my presence caused the Gray-breasted Jays to withdraw, but the Sulphur-belly seemed as oblivious to me as the mother trogon. The Sulphur-belly Flycatcher only quit the assault when, after repeated attempts over a quarter of an hour, it could not separate the parent bird from her baby.

Juveniles

As summer rolls into August, both adult and juvenile Elegant Trogons become increasingly silent. Territories dissolve as pairs roam the canyons searching for enough food to support their ravenous young. "Thick with Fruit" is the Chiricahua Apache name for the harvest period in late summer and early fall. Members of a tropical family of fruit-eaters, Arizona trogons turn their attention almost exclusively to berries after the young leave the nest. Birchleaf Buckthorn fruits are the first to be exploited, but, as they become scarce, the trogon family switches to Canyon Grape and Southwest Chokecherry. Fortunately, a variety of fruits are available to satisfy the appetite of the rapidly-growing fledglings.

The young are utterly dependent upon their parents during these first few weeks. Bob-tailed and short-winged, their flight is slow and awkward. They often miss target perches. Seldom do they fly to positions over 20 feet above the ground, and, not uncommonly, they choose boughs less than five feet in height. Aside from feeding them, the adults must also teach their progeny to flee from danger. Juveniles are surprisingly tame. If no adult is present to sound the alarm *W-kkkk*, young Elegants allow squirrels and people to come within 10 feet, only gazing curiously at them. They seem to feel invisible in their mottled, neutral-colored plumage.

Approaching their first month out of the nest—and with almost no success—the fledglings begin making their own foraging attempts on berries. I've seen young birds rip off leaves trying to catch a buckthorn berry. Often they try to swallow the foliage before dropping it. Once I saw a juvenile Elegant Trogon reposition an oak twig in its bill that was an exact match for the walkingsticks being brought to it by the adults. It was minutes before it finally seemed to realize that it had not caught an insect.

With the acquisition of a full length tail at about one month of age, the young begin to molt into their first coat of sexually dimorphic plumage. But even as the backs of young males turn emerald and those of hatching-year females change to a soft shade of cinnamon, they retain the off-yellow rows of spots on the wing coverts that identify them as birds of the year. Perhaps to defuse aggression from the male parent, the young males still possess the white teardrop behind the eye and the heavily barred undertail characteristic of adult females.

Departure

I have encountered spot-winged juveniles as early as the first week of June and as late as mid-October. Regardless when they leave the nest, most Elegant Trogon families seem to disappear from Arizona during autumn. This is the time of the year the Apaches call "Earth is Reddish-Brown."

Trees continue to develop fruit in the fall, Netleaf Hackberry and Arizona Madrone, but the nights have turned cool in the mile-high world of the border canyons. Scarlet Sumac and Poison Ivy flare briefly in early September, then drop their leaves. By October, red tongues of Virginia Creeper barber stripe sycamore trees and Velvet Ash burns with waxy yellow light in the riparian woodland. Every afternoon Indian summer paints the towering cliffs of Cave Creek with butterscotch alpenglow.

The last few trogons feed voraciously in preparation for departure. Full-grown young with rose pink abdomens are nearly as spectacular as their parents as the whole family executes short diving flights to harvest small, dry fruits from a Canyon Grape. Given a moon, the group may be gone from the canyon by morning. Ordinarily, no Elegant Trogons remain in the Chiricahua Mountains after the first week of November.

Years ago, I met a rancher with a spread in the broad grasslands of the Sulphur Springs Valley, on the west side of the Chiricahuas. After he learned of my interest in birds, he told me about a beautiful Scissor-tailed Flycatcher he had seen down at his corrals one cold November day. He even had a photograph. The bird in the picture was an adult female Elegant Trogon. My guess is she was fattening up on the pyracantha berries growing by his house.

The late Alexander Clay told me he saw a male Elegant Trogon on the San Pedro River at the foot of the Huachuca Mountains in 1979. In recent years, late fall sightings of trogons in the cottonwood groves along the San Pedro have almost become an annual event. Winter sightings also continue to accumulate. Single birds, especially females, seem increasingly content to endure the cold in the dense riparian cover on lower Sonoita Creek, below Peña Blanca Lake, or in lower Sycamore Canyon of the Atascosas. Judging from the scarcity of records, however, most of Arizona's trogons cross into Mexico in one long flight.

No one knows how far south they migrate. No one knows whether most follow the mountain cordilleras or the winding rivers in the valleys. Certainly, Elegant Trogons occur on the Río Cuchujaqui in southernmost Sonora in midwinter; on recent Christmas counts for the Alamos area, the number has varied from four to 29. Since Elegants, as a species, have a remarkably stable population dynamic, it seems reasonable to speculate that a wave of northern migrants augments the resident group in midwinter some years. But no one knows if these birds originate from Arizona.

"Ghost Face" is the Apache name for the last season of the year. All winter long, birders will continue to visit the border canyons, even in the bleakest weather, gathering over mugs of hot coffee and open field guides at places like the Portal Store, the Ramsey Canyon Preserve, and the Santa Rita Lodge. They talk about the birds they've seen that day. Eventually, conversations turn to the species that no one is likely to see or hear till April.

When the Apache wheel comes full circle to "Many Leaves," it will be time to listen again for the harsh *Koa's* of a crimson-breasted male heralding the arrival of a new year. Then, like so many others, I will return to the deep canyons of the Arizona borderlands. The bird I will most want to see is the beautiful Elegant Trogon.

Photograph by Richard Taylor

*Fledgling Elegant Trogon,
first day after leaving the nest.*

Photograph by Richard Taylor

*Female Elegant Trogon
feeding Birchleaf Buckthorn
fruit to new fledgling.*

Photograph by Richard Taylor

*Fledgling Elegant Trogon,
10 days after leaving nest. Note
"teardrop" mark behind eye.*

Photograph by Richard Taylor

*Adult and young male Elegant
Trogons. Young trogons retain
off-white spots on the wing
coverts for the first winter.*

*Adult male Elegant Trogon
with walkingstick. Angle of
refraction makes back appear
blue, because the color is
structural, not pigment.*

*Adult female Elegant Trogon.
Trogons possess ability to rotate
head 180 degrees.*

Photograph by Richard Taylor

Photograph by Richard Taylor

Photograph by Richard Taylor

*Trogon habitat: South Fork Cave Creek, Chiricahua Mountains,
in November. Both Elegant and Eared Trogons use this
grove of Arizona sycamore and bigtooth maple.*

Photograph by Richard Taylor

Adult male Elegant Trogon.

The first Eared Trogon discovered in Arizona in October, 1977.
Notice the atypical mostly black tail.

X
A Trogon Ethos

*E*legant Trogons return to their breeding grounds in the borderland canyons of Southeastern Arizona starting in mid-April, in most years. While the primary goal of some bird-watchers making the pilgrimage to these areas may be another neotropical species—the Zone-tailed Hawk, Sulphur-bellied Flycatcher, Rose-throated Becard, or the Painted Redstart—at least 50,000 come each year hoping to glimpse the resplendent plumage of the Elegant Trogon.

A dozen individual birds, those that are most accessible, support almost the full weight of this human landslide. Formerly, only the California Condor and the Whooping Crane commanded comparable attention in the United States. Few other populations of wildlife are as economically important or give so much aesthetic pleasure to man.

To assure the future of Arizona's Elegant Trogon, I propose the following rules of conduct abstracted from the biology of the species:

Do not use tape recorders or other sound devices to attract trogons.

It is completely unnecessary. The spring and summer calls of the Elegant Trogon are louder than most other bird voices in the pine-oak woodland. Because dense vegetation characterizes their habitat, trogons rely on antiphonal vocalizations—duetting—to attract a mate, to establish territories, and to

Trogon—one day after fledging

maintain the pair bond. Males share incubation and feeding duties with the female. Virtually every component of trogon breeding ecology is dependent on the sound environment, and any auditory disruption undermines the chances for a self-regenerating U.S. population.

Always use a blind to photograph a nest.

More known nest failures can be directly attributed to thoughtless photographers than any other cause. As insectivores which take their prey on the wing, trogons are equipped with very sharp eyes. They show extreme reluctance to adopt nests under human surveillance. Once committed to a clutch, either adult may refuse its turn at incubation if people are present; later on, nestlings may be abandoned altogether if the visual disturbance is prolonged.

Never clip screening vegetation or break limbs that interfere with a clear view of the nest cavity.

An acceptable nest must have a nearby bare branch for a perch.

Never rap, scratch, or tap known or suspected nest trees.

This causes nest abandonment. Although there is variation between pairs, trogons are typically upset by any activity within 75 feet of their nest.

Back off when trogons sound their alarm call.

A *W-kkkk*, which begins sharply and trails into a series of chucks, is the trogon alarm call. Male trogons have a reputation in some quarters as curious birds. During the foresummer, especially, they tend to investigate anyone that intrudes on their territories. Bisyllabic challenges of *Koa* often accompany these confrontations. But when either sex utters their shrill alarm, the birds are extremely disturbed. You have encroached on the nest zone, or fledglings are hidden nearby. Retreat. If you wait patiently at a respectable distance, you may be rewarded with both memorable views and firsthand insights into the ecology of the Elegant Trogon.

Walk quietly when visiting trogon haunts.

Most of the major canyons of the border ranges are penetrated by roads up to the 6,000 foot level, originally engineered as tracks for miners and fuelwood cutters. If the canyon gradient was mild enough to permit the passage of primitive machinery, it probably also traps sufficient nutrients and water to support big sycamores, oaks, and pines. Here—not road's end—is where the trogons are. The Nature Conservancy has wisely set the example by asking birdwatchers to walk in Ramsey Canyon of the Huachuca Mountains.

If people will only show this much courtesy, a new, mutually beneficial era of human-Elegant Trogon relations will begin in the borderland canyons of Southeastern Arizona.

Literature Consulted

Allen, A. A. 1944. An Arizona nest of the Elegant Trogon. *Auk* 61: 640-642.

_____1944. Touring for birds. *National Geographic Magazine* 85:689.

American Birds. 1978. Female trogon at Bentsen, Rio Grande Valley. Vol. 32: 229.

Bailey, F. M. 1923. Birds recorded from the Santa Rita Mountains in southern Arizona. Cooper Ornithological Club, *Pacific Coast Avifauna* 15.

Balda, R. P. 1965. The birds of the Chiricahua Mountains, Arizona. Unpublished doctoral dissertation. University of Illinois, Chicago.

Bent, A. C. 1939. Life histories of North American woodpeckers. Smithsonian Institute, United States National Museum Bulletin 174.

_____1940. Life histories of North American cuckoos, goatsuckers, hummingbirds and their allies. Smithsonian Institute, United States National Museum Bulletin 176.

Bishop, R. A. 1964. The Mearn's Quail in southern Arizona. Unpublished master's thesis. University of Arizona, Tucson.

Brandt, H. 1951. *Arizona and Its Birdlife.* The Bird Research Foundation. Cleveland, Ohio.

Brown, D. E. 1973. Western range extensions of Scaled Quail, Montezuma Quail and Elegant Trogon in Arizona. *Western Birds* 4:59.

Goodding, L. N. 1946. A hidden botanical garden. *New York Botanical Garden Journal* 47:86-96.

Graham, F. 1979. Case of the ugly birder. *Audubon* 81, No. 4:88-100.

Granger, B. H., ed. 1960. *Arizona Place Names.* University of Arizona Press, Tucson.

Hastings, J. R. and R. M. Turner. 1965. *The Changing Mile.* University of Arizona Press, Tucson.

Hinde, R. A., ed. 1969. Bird vocalizations: Their relations to current problems in biology and psychology. Cambridge University Press. New York, NY.

Hubbard, J. P. 1972. Notes on Arizona birds. *Nemouria* 51-22.

Jackman, S. M. and J. M. Scott. 1975. Literature review of twenty-three selected forest birds of the Pacific Northwest. Region 6, U.S. Forest Service files.

Kaufmann, J. H., Lanning, D. V., and S. E. Poole. 1976. Current status and distribution of the Coati in the United States. *Journal of Mammalogy* 57: 621-637.

Lack, D. 1943. *The Life of the Robin.* H. F. & G. Witherby, London.

Leopold, A. S. 1959. Wildlife of Mexico, the game birds and mammals. University of California Press, Berkeley.

Ligon, J. D. 1968. Sexual differences in foraging behavior in two species of dendrocopos woodpeckers. *Auk* 85:203-215.

Little, E. L., Jr. 1950. Southwestern trees. U.S. Department of Agriculture. Agriculture Handbook No. 9.

Marshall, Joe T., Jr. 1957. Birds of pine-oak woodland in southern Arizona and adjacent Mexico. Cooper Ornithological Society, *Pacific Coast Avifauna* 32.

Marshall, Judy and R. P. Balda. 1974. The breeding ecology of the Painted Redstart. *Condor* 76:89-101; *Arizona Highways* 26, No. 3:4-9.

Mills, G. S. 1977. New locations for the Five-striped Sparrow in the United States. *Western Birds* 8:121-130.

Olsen, S. J. and J. W. Olsen. 1974. The macaws of grasshopper ruin. *The Kiva* 40:67-70.

Peterson, R. T. and E. L. Chalif. 1973. *A Field Guide to Mexican Birds.* Houghton Mifflin Company, Boston.

Phillips, A., Marshall, J. and G. Monson. 1964. *The Birds of Arizona.* University of Arizona Press, Tucson.

Ridgway, R. 1911. The birds of North and Middle America: part V. United States National Museum Bulletin 50.

Scott, V. E Evans, K. E., Patton, D. R and C. P. Stone. 1977. Cavity-nesting birds of North American forests. U S Department of Agriculture. Agriculture Handbook No. 511.

Scott, W. E. D. 1886. On the avi-fauna of Pinal County, with remarks on some birds of Pima and Gila Counties, Arizona. *Auk* 3:425.

Skutch, A. F. 1942. Life history of the Mexican Trogon. *Auk* 59:341-363.

Stebbins, R. C. 1966. *Field Guide to Western Reptiles and Amphibians.* Houghton Mifflin Company, Boston.

Steele, E. 1966. Arizona's mystery bird. *Audubon* 68:167-170.

Swarth, H. S. 1904. Birds of the Huachuca Mountains, Arizona. Cooper Ornithological Club, *Pacific Coast Avifauna* 4.

Taylor, C. 1977. *Hiking Trails and Wilderness Routes of the Chiricahua Mountains.* Rainbow Expeditions, Tucson.

_____1978. A trogon ethos. Tucson Audubon Society *Vermilion Flycatcher.* April:16-17.

_____1979. Huachuca Mountain trogon day census. Huachuca Audubon Society *Trogon News* 6, No. 4:2.

Thornberg, R. and F. Thornberg. 1950. Some interesting visitors. *Arizona Highways* 26, No. 3:4-9.

Toolin L. J., Van Devender, T. R. and J. M. Kaiser. 1979. The flora of Sycamore Canyon, Santa Cruz County, Arizona. University of Arizona, Tucson. Department of Geosciences Publication 840.

Tremontano, J. P. 1964. Comparative studies of the Rock Wren and the Canyon Wren. Unpublished master's thesis. University of Arizona, Tucson.

U.S. Forest Service. No date. Goodding Research Natural Area. Coronado National Forest, Tucson.

van Rossem, A. J. 1936. Notes on birds in relation to faunal areas of south-central Arizona. Transactions of the San Diego Society of Natural History 8:121-148.

Welty J. C. 1975. *The Life of Birds.* W. B. Saunders Company, Philadelphia, PA.

Zimmerman, D. A. 1978. Eared Trogon—immigrant or visitor? *American Birds* 32:135-139.

The Eared Trogon
in Arizona

Introduction

At two o'clock in the afternoon on October 23, 1977, in the South Fork of Cave Creek Canyon of the Chiricahua Mountains, Arizona, I saw the first Eared Trogon ever reported in the United States. I was winding up my first season of research on the Elegant Trogon when I heard the unusual, almost musical calls.

The trogon was peering over its shoulder at me. I immediately looked for the white tear drop behind the eye which identifies Elegant Trogon juveniles and adult females. There was no teardrop, and—to my surprise—there was no orange eye-ring. Furthermore, the bill of this bird was slate gray, *not* yellow.

While the realization swept over me that I was looking at an entirely new species of trogon, the bird launched itself across the canyon, uttering yet another cry novel to me. I remember thinking it was a male because of its iridescent green back, still unable to disassociate it from the familiar Elegant. Working my way down the creek minutes later, the bird revealed its location with a loud squeal. For the next 30 seconds, I got my first full frontal view of the newcomer.

There was *no* white collar separating the brilliant red belly and breast from the green upper torso. The undertail was nearly all black, except for two white crescents entering midway on either outer edge. The undertail was *not* barred. Abruptly the bird was airborne, flashing dazzling white outer tail feathers as it gave its flight call. I followed it from perch to perch for the next two hours.

Totally missing was the bullheaded, *macho* jizz of *Trogon elegans*. The trogon was big—Band-tailed Pigeon-sized—yet its head and bill were small compared to the Elegant. The upper surface of its tail was entirely blue—police-suit blue. Tails of male Elegant Trogon are olive green with a black terminal band. In profile, its wings were dark, with a rich brown luster in good light, and its wing coverts were the same metallic green as its back. Both wings and wing coverts of the Elegant Trogon are smoke gray.

As striking as its structural were its behavioral distinctions. Elegant Trogons feed in the lower third of the streamside forest; the new trogon foraged exclusively in the upper half. Elegant Trogons had become nearly silent; the new trogon announced every flight with a loud *Kac-ka-k-kac*, every perch with a series of *wEEE-ks* accented by a powerful tail pump. Elegant Trogons had long since become accustomed to human pressure in South Fork, but the new trogon proved impossible to approach within 50 yards before it flew. The upshot was I escorted the bird 1.5 miles down South Fork before it doubled back. In an entire research season, I had never seen Elegant Trogons fly half as far before taking evasive action.

Kim Innes, a graduate student from Cornell University, was with me when the trogon flew vertically 150 feet up a cliff face to a perch in a half-dead pinyon pine. Then it launched itself up the South Fork Road, flying with the undulatory motion of the family, nearly twice the height of the canopy below. I had never seen an Elegant Trogon fly so high nor risk such great exposure to hawks.

Kim confirmed details of the bird's appearance and told me that she had heard its strange cries for nearly a week. That reminded me of a conversation I'd had several days earlier with Ruth Morse, Assistant Director of the Southwestern Research Station. Ruth had both seen and heard a *blue-tailed* trogon *squealing* in the North Fork of Cave Creek as far back as October 15th.

But the bird's identity remained a mystery. Kim offered me a lift to my car, and from there we sped down to the Portal Ranger Station to telephone Vince Roth, Director of the Southwestern Research Station. He copied down my description and called back 10 minutes later. According to *A Field Guide to Mexican Birds*, I had seen a male Eared Trogon with an atypical undertail. After consulting my own Peterson and Chalif, I agreed. The Eared Trogon, *Euptilotis neoxenus*, had been added to the list of United States avifauna.

Background

Before the black-tailed, South Fork male vanished after a five weeks stay on December 3, 1977, it was joined by three other Eared Trogons. Additionally, December 1, 1977, Betty Jones spotted a male Eared Trogon in Ramsey Canyon of the Huachuca Mountains. It, too, disappeared after December 3rd. This account summarizes what is known of the population and ecology of Eared Trogons in Arizona today, 15 years after their first appearance.

Between October 23, 1977 and November 30, 1977, I had the opportunity to observe the South Fork Eared Trogons on 15 separate days. Since then, I have been fortunate enough to encounter them several more times in both the Chiricahua and the Huachuca Mountains. Through the kindness of Sheri Williamson, co-manager of the Ramsey Canyon Nature Preserve, I even joined the nest monitoring program she devised for the first known breeding attempt of an Eared Trogon in the United States.

In January, 1983, I saw my first Eared Trogon in Mexico at Barranca Rancho Liebre in the state of Sinaloa, Mexico. In 1985, I began leading birding tours to Barranca del Cobre in Chihuahua, Mexico, approximately 325 airline miles southeast of Cave Creek Canyon in the Chiricahua Mountains. Since learning their likely haunts, I have seen Eared Trogons in northern

Mexico at least twice annually, and some years more frequently. Much of my personal information comes from watching the Eared Trogons of Barranca del Cobre.

Additionally, I've had the good fortune to observe 14 other species of trogons and four species of quetzals in Mexico, Central America, and South America. Knowledge of the family as a whole has enriched my appreciation of the Eared Trogon. This species is big, unique, and rare. In a group renowned for beauty, the Eared Trogon is among the most beautiful. But I think the true reason I remain so fascinated by this species is because so little is known about its life history. Of all the birds that inhabit the Arizona border mountains, Eared Trogon is undoubtedly the most mysterious.

History & Distribution

The furor the first Eared Trogon created among the ranks of U.S. birders was considerable. Recorded north from the Sierra Madre of Michoacán to central Chihuahua, a span of about 900 airline miles, the Eared Trogon has the most restricted distribution of any of the nine species of Mexican trogons. The area it inhabits is perhaps the wildest mountain terrain in Mexico, and it is rare or uncommon throughout its range. In 1977, it seemed nothing short of incredible that one should show up north of the international boundary. But the few records from Chihuahua and Sonora suggest that the Eared Trogon had been poised to enter the U.S. for over half a century.

In 1911, Robert Ridgway published a report of an Eared Trogon in northern Chihuahua, just 95 miles below the border at Colonia Garcia, and only 125 miles from the Chiricahua Mountains. Joe T. Marshall recorded *Euptilotis* on his study plots at 6,750 feet elevation on the Río Gavilán in August, 1952, 133 miles below the Chiricahuas. Again in June of 1953, Marshall found the species about 150 miles away in the Sierra de Nácori Chico.

Prior to 1977, the northernmost Mexico record was only 115 miles away from the Chiricahuas. On June 1, 1956, Allen R. Phillips heard an Eared Trogon calling in the Sierra Huachinera, Sonora.

For all of these sites, the direct line flight distance to Ramsey Canyon in the Huachuca Mountains is only approximately five miles further. Obviously, neither the distance to the Chiricahuas or to the Huachucas was an insurmountable gap for a large bird like the Eared Trogon.

In 1977, many wondered if the Ramsey Canyon trogon recorded on December 1 had simply flown in from the Chiricahuas, 75 miles away. In spite of the huge visitation the Huachucas experience, December 3, 1977, marked the last time Eared Trogon was seen or heard in the Huachuca Mountains till August 6, 1984 when Robert T. Smith—"Smitty"— saw one in Scheelite Canyon. Three years later, on August 9, 1989, David Sibley spotted an Eared Trogon near Comfort Spring at the head of Carr Canyon. Ramsey Canyon lies midway between Scheelite and Carr Canyons. A week afterwards, I traversed the length of Ramsey Canyon, looking and listening for Eared Trogons. I found nothing.

Sue Perger, a member of The Nature Conservancy staff in Ramsey Canyon, discovered the next Eared Trogons in the Huachuca Mountains. Hiking above the Ramsey Box on August 6, 1991 with John Porter, a herpetologist, she recognized the calls of Eared Trogons before she saw them. The pair she found were the same birds that produced the first U.S. nest of the Eared Trogon just two months later.

Meanwhile, sightings from the Chiricahua Mountains continued to trickle in. Robert J. Morse chronicled the occurrence of Eared Trogons in South Fork Cave Creek in an article published in the October 1987 issue of *Birding* magazine. At that time, *Euptilotis* had appeared in South Fork seven of the 11 years since 1977. No observations were recorded from the Chiricahuas in 1988, but, since then, there have been multiple sightings annually. Aside from South Fork, Eared Trogons have been seen in the intervening years in the main canyon of Cave Creek, and on the west side of the Chiricahuas in both Pinery Canyon and Rock Creek. The evidence suggests that breeding Eared Trogons also occur in the Chiricahua Mountains.

The most recent border range to see an Eared Trogon has been the Santa Rita Mountains. On August 7, 1991, Rich Stallcup encountered a pair high on the slopes of Madera Canyon. Across the crest of the mountains two weeks later, Troy Corman found a lone female in upper Gardner Canyon. For the sake of comparison, it took Elegant Trogons 33 years at the turn of the century to bridge the gap between the Huachuca and Santa Ritas Mountains. Eared Trogons covered the identical span in just 14 years.

More remarkable, Dan Fischer spotted an Eared Trogon on central Arizona's Black River on June 13, 1992. Black River is a leap of yet another 115 miles from the species' previous northernmost outpost in the Chiricahuas. Clearly, Eared Trogons have the physical capacity to make protracted flights—regardless of whether they originate from Arizona or northern Mexico. Given its potential for additional population recruitment, it seems certain that Eared Trogons have come to the U.S. to stay.

Taxonomy

Eared Trogons belong to a monotypic genus presently sandwiched between the five species of quetzals and the 17 species of true trogons found on the mainland in the western hemisphere. *Euptilotis neoxenus* (literally, "hairy-eared new stranger") was the last trogon to be described from Mexico in 1838. It takes its genus from several long, filamentous auriculars, or "ear" feathers that begin below and behind the eye and contour horizontally around the hind head. Although they may extend one-quarter to three-eighths inch beyond the head, these wispy, hair-like tufts are invisible under normal field conditions.

It owes the last half of its scientific name to a unique morphology. With a torso only one inch shorter than the Resplendent Quetzal's, Eared Trogons are the second longest member of the family in Mexico and Central America. The silhouette of an Eared Trogon—little head, large body, and long wings—is a dead ringer for that of a female quetzal. Male Eareds cannot match the hemispherical golden crest that is the glory of male Resplendents, but, like quetzals, *Euptilotis* lacks a serration or "tooth" on its upper mandible. Its bill is the most delicate of all the New World trogons. Like all species of quetzals, female Eareds have iridescent green backs. Females of no other genus of trogon have this stunning iridescence. Like quetzals, both sexes of Eared Trogons have glowing green wing coverts. All other trogons have dull black, black and white, or gray wing coverts.

But the Eared's big, disc-shaped wing coverts are not elongated into the ornamental frieze that distinguishes the five quetzal species in the world. And, of course, the Eared Trogon lacks the fabulous train of uppertail coverts that extend at least the length of the tail in all male quetzals, trailing three full feet beyond the tail tip in the case of the Resplendent Quetzal. Covering about 55 percent of the tail—it should be mentioned in fairness—the leaf-shaped uppertail coverts of Eared Trogon are exceeded in length only by those of quetzals. Even by trogon family standards, they are impressive.

Unlike the dull black central tail tract of all quetzals, the same feathers in the tails of Eared Trogons are glossy blue. But the *shape* of the Eared's tail is exactly like a quetzal's: it tapers. The tail tips of all 17 species of true trogons in the West are conspicuously square; many of them actually flare.

In fact, *Euptilotis neoxenus* seems to represent the evolutionary precursor to *Pharomachrus*, the genus to which all the world's quetzals are assigned. Or did Eared Trogon and Resplendent Quetzal arise from a common ancestor and simply choose different evolutionary paths? Are the "ear" tufts an incipient corona, or are they the vestigial crest of a bygone era? These are questions future taxonomists will be asked to answer.

Indisputably, a glimpse of an Eared Trogon—big, red-breasted, seemingly throwing off wavelengths of aquamarine, snow white tail flashing as it crosses a wilderness canyon in Arizona—this spectacle must rank among the most electrifying birding experiences available in all North America.

Identification

Except for birds of prey, Common Ravens, or a possible Wild Turkey, Eared Trogons are among the largest birds of the upper elevations of the Arizona border ranges. Both sexes are about 13 inches long. They are almost exactly the same length as a female Sharp-shinned Hawk or a Band-tailed Pigeon, and an inch longer than the Rock Doves of our city parks. Comparatively, they seem a magnitude larger than Elegant Trogons, and, weighing approximately 100 grams, they are about half again as heavy.

In Arizona, they can be distinguished from Elegants of either gender at any age by their dainty, slate-colored bill, and by the absence of a bold eye-ring. Additionally, neither sex has a white breast band. Their tails are rich blue on the backside, and the white outer tail feathers show from the rear and are conspicuous in flight. Typically, both sexes have unmarked wide, white undertails that taper to a black terminal band. The black tip is actually formed by the six central rectrices which project half an inch or better beyond the translucent white undertail tract. Black at their base, these six feathers maximize contrast on the undertail.

Seen from the rear, the entire back and upper tail coverts of either sex are deep metallic green with subtle blue hues in oblique lighting. The rump is more apt to show azure than the upper back. Long and well-defined, the uppertail coverts extend slightly more than half the length of the lustrous blue tail. The lower breast and belly of both sexes is fire engine red, not the pure crimson of an Elegant Trogon, noticeably a shade more orange. Wings are dark with a chestnut gloss on the primaries, and the wing coverts are iridescent green. Usually hidden or inconspicuous, both their short tarsi and their feet are slate-colored. In other respects, Eared Trogons are different enough to allow observers to sex and age them in the field.

Adult Male: The small head of the male is dull black, as are its throat and neck. Its black hood fuses with the iridescent green breast in front; on the back there is a cleanly demarcated change to deep green. The hair-like auriculars are almost never observed, but in strong light, there may be wavy silver markings behind the eyes. These gossamer lines are, conceivably, highlights from the sun on the ear feather tract.

Adult Female: The head of an adult female is medium gray—distinctly lighter than the adult male's. Its upper breast and throat is brownish-gray or fawn-colored. The female also has the hair-like "ears" that distinguish the species. Back, wings, and tail are all as in the male.

Juvenile Male: The head is charcoal-colored, lighter than the black of an adult male. Iridescent green breast plumage identifies it as a male, in spite of its lighter head. The juvenile male observed in November 1977 had a half dozen brownish, rust-colored spots on the breast, above, below, and actually on the color division. Its breast and belly were more orange than either of the adults.

Juvenile Female: The head of the juvenile female is slightly darker gray than the neck and both are a lighter shade than the adult female's. Like the adult female, her breast is pearly-gray or fawn-colored, but its orange-red belly only extends two-thirds up to shoulder, not level with the shoulder as in the other three birds described. The interior lining of its bill is a deep orange-red, and probably this is also true for the juvenile male.

Fledgling: Spotted wing covert tips loosely arranged in several rows on the "shoulders" of the young birds is a family trait shared by all fledgling trogons and quetzals. When Sheri Williamson examined the nestlings from the failed Ramsey Canyon nest, she noted these spots were conspicuous buff-white against black wings. Another character fledgling Eareds have in common with young Elegants is a mottled breast and belly. In most other respects, including the luminous blue tail, Eared Trogons resemble the adult female parent for their first month out of the nest. Unlike young Elegants, Eared Trogons have no apostrophe of white behind the eye.

Vocalizations

As with other members of their family, Eared Trogons are almost impossible to find unless they call. The iridescence of their ultramarine-green plumage is structural, not pigment; in shade, the color of an Eared Trogon dies to a neutral tone somewhere between moss green and soot gray. They simply blend with with the background of the pine-fir world they inhabit. Only when they call are they apt to reveal their immaculate white tails and flame red breasts. Moreover, their calls give birders insight into the mood of the bird. Understanding the meaning of the four basic vocalizations will tell the birder to back off or approach.

wEEE-k: A vehement squeal abruptly ending with a *chuck* sound, usually delivered several times in succession and each typically accompanied by an upward flick of the tail lasting approximately one second. This call, given while the bird perches, reminds me of the alarm call of Elegant Trogons (*w-kkk*) and of a similar cry (*wec-wec*) used by Resplendent Quetzals. In all three species, the cry is associated with tail pumping, and its purpose seems to be to warn others of its kind visually—as well as audibly—of an intruder's presence. The squeal-chuck is the single loudest bird call in the border canyons when Eared Trogons are present. It is used by both sexes and it can be heard by humans up to 400 yards away. In Arizona, it is usually the birder that has prompted the vocalization, although in Mexico, it often seems directed at another Eared Trogon that has trespassed on the first bird's territory. Birders should avoid attempting to approach closer than 50 yards when a bird is using the squeal-chuck.

Weee: A cry only used by pairs, often repeatedly by one or both birds, it appears to locate the birds for each other. This half-second-long contact note reminds me of a single violin stroke, others of a squeaky door hinge. While the call always seems loud, the bird giving the call can be deceptively near the observer, possibly indicating that the volume of the cry is variable. I have walked right under a tree where an Eared Trogon sat using this call without causing it to fly.

Kac-ka-k-kac: The sharp, cackling flight call given by both sexes, uttered rapidly—usually several times—as the bird launches itself. This call probably locates the direction of flight for other Eared Trogons. Outspread tail rectrices with flashing white visible both above and below reinforces the signal during flight. I don't believe I've ever seen an Eared Trogon fly that failed to use the flight call if disturbed, even when it seemed no other Eared Trogon was present.

Tremolo: Dale A. Zimmerman's term for a protracted series of bisyllabic whistles that begin softly and ascend in volume till they are as loud as an eagle call. Apparently, they are the Eared Trogon's mating song. This is the call most apt to be heard from April through August. From September through March, the song is used infrequently and seems related to resource or territorial defense. Eared Trogons are almost oblivious to humans while using the tremolo; they may move toward a birder, rather than away, if she or he remains quiet.

Territory & Behavior

Many birdwatchers have learned the will-o'-the-wisp nature of most Eared Trogon sightings. The birds are spotted for a single day, then they vanish. The next sighting may be the next day, the next week, or the following year. It may come from miles up the same canyon, or an adjacent drainage, or even another mountain range. Clearly, Eared Trogons are strong fliers. With wings exceeding their tails in length, *Euptilotis* is far more mobile than the familiar Elegant Trogon of the boundary mountains.

On my first encounter with an Eared Trogon in the fall of 1977, the bird flew 1.5 miles. Nothing in my research of the smaller Elegant had prepared me for a trogon that would choose evasion over concealment. The following morning, I located the same bird almost two miles higher up South Fork than the previous evening. After one week of unrelenting pursuit by over 200 birders, it was using an area three full miles above South Fork Campground. Then it disappeared. Finally, 12 days later, it resurfaced in the original madrone grove where I had first seen it. Therefore, the total *known* range of the adult male with a black tail was a stretch of South Fork 3.5 miles long.

Even more remarkable was the case of the male Eared Trogon spotted by Pete Dunne and Robert Morse in South Fork June 21, 1989. By a stroke of good fortune, the same bird was probably refound by Rick Plage and Chuck Rau the next day in the adjacent Snowshed Fork of Cave Creek Canyon. Assuming it was the same individual, this bird flew over 1,000-foot-high Snowshed Ridge—a direct line distance of no less than 3.5 miles.

In his classic *Birds of Pine-Oak Woodland*, published in 1957 by the Cooper Ornithological Society, Joe T. Marshall wrote that a pair in the Sierra Madre "crosses a mile of forage area daily and ceremoniously returns over the same route at dusk." Marshall was watching Eared Trogon behavior during the summer when he made the following observations:

> A lone male traveled about two miles along a ridge three times a day; his conspicuous song and large territory contrasted with those of a pair inspecting tree holes near camp. The latter birds sang only when this male came near. Another bird sang two miles farther down the same ridge of forest-like Apache Pines. Thus there were three singing males in as many miles . . .

In 1977, a second pair of juvenile Eared Trogons arrived in South Fork on November 13. They had a lineal range along the canyon bottom of 4.6 miles for the three weeks they were present. The ranges of the adult pair and the juvenile pair overlapped 2.1 miles. With the exception of times when three Eared Trogons were observed together, always two males and one female, the adult birds always occupied a higher portion of the canyon than the subadults. Altogether, the Eared Trogons ranged over a six-mile length of Cave Creek Canyon and South Fork in the fall of 1977.

Given their large territories, the daily movements of Eared Trogons may be surprisingly circumscribed. On each of six separate visits to South Fork between November 23 and 30, 1977, I was able to locate the pair of juveniles over a 0.3 mile stretch of canyon bottom where madrone flourished. From 10:00 a.m. to 5:00 p.m. on November 26, Richard Todd of the Arizona Game & Fish Department and I viewed the birds almost continuously. Throughout the day, they foraged over an area only 0.2 mile long. At 5:00 p.m., in the dim autumn twilight of the deep canyon, they became invisible in the dense foliage of a tall Douglas fir. They probably roosted there overnight.

Paired Eared Trogons communicate frequently, especially using the musical *Weee* cry, and usually stay within 50 yards of one another, often much less. When they fly, they invariably use the piercing *Kac-ka-k-kac* call. Many times they perch in the same tree, and often on the same branch. Perches are typically in the upper third of a conifer on bare, broad boughs, although once I saw a bird drop down to a piece of driftwood in the creekbed, below the level of the adjoining banks. Rose Ann Rowlett, on a successful quest for Eared Trogons in the Sierra Madre in 1971, also observed a pair go down to the ground "on a piney ridgetop" in Durango, Mexico.

When perched, Eared Trogons usually assume a peculiar hunched position with their lower backs humped up like a dowager's bustle. Since Eareds prefer branches about two inches thick, this posture may enable them to push backwards off their perch with a minimum of effort. I've seen the same position used often by Resplendent Quetzals and even, occasionally, by Elegant Trogons.

Food

Throughout the autumn of 1977, the four Eared Trogons in South Fork concentrated on the heavy crop of madrone berries. Here the madrones grow in distinct groves, and the trogons passed most of their time in these groves. When the madrone trees were finally stripped bare in early December, the Eared Trogons disappeared.

Berries were seized from the crown foliage of madrones in short, buoyant flights that often began and ended in the same tree. The birds hovered briefly as they seized the fruit, then flew to nearby perches. Feeding usually occurred in bursts of activity lasting five to 10 minutes. After feeding, the birds became lethargic, unless stressed, assuming perches for an hour or longer. Pairs of trogons remained in one madrone grove for days at a time, apparently reluctant to abandon these rich food sources.

The Eared Trogons I've seen in Mexico have specialized on arthropods and larvae. Infrequently, Eareds hawk their prey, flying nearly straight up to seize insects too small to be visible, then returning to the same or a nearby perch. Once I saw a trogon use the identical perch in a madrone tree for hawking insects three times in succession. More often, Eareds capture woolly black caterpillars, green larvae, and katydids in spectacular swooping flights with their flashing tails widespread. Sometimes they even "barber stripe" a tree, fluttering in a tight spiral down around a trunk. Fanning their tails in this situation may spook dinner out of hiding and help make it easier to catch.

Rose Ann Rowlett described the same dramatic feeding spiral for a male she observed in late July of 1971 in the Sierra Madre of Durango, Mexico. Here, too, a pair of Eared Trogons concentrated much of their foraging time on a fruiting madrone.

Moved by birds he watched in the Sierra Madre during the summers of 1952 and 1953, Marshall wrote:

> The magnificent Eared Trogon gleans arthropods from pine foliage while hovering an instant with body vertical; then it falls, levels off, and flies to a bare horizontal branch. . . Nearly all the activity I saw took place at middle height in tall pines; flights are above the intervening oaks.

The word "magnificent" eclipses the science for anyone who has the chance to watch Eared Trogons in action.

Competition

On the afternoon of November 17, 1977, only minutes after seeing my first female Eared Trogon, I saw the male attacked and driven up a tributary of South Fork in the Chiricahuas by an adult male Elegant Trogon. The female Eared accompanied her mate. So, in essence, a single Elegant Trogon was able to drive two larger birds of the same family what turned out to be a full quarter mile. The Elegant Trogon seemed faster than its larger relative, and it attacked by flying from lower perches upward at its adversary. The male Eared Trogon always abandoned its perch. I never saw any actual physical contact.

The Eared Trogons complained loudly throughout the conflict, repeatedly uttering the *wEEE-k* cry as well as the shrill flight cackle. This contrasted with the murderous silence of the attacking Elegant Trogon. Pursuit was abandoned by the Elegant Trogon only when the Eared Trogons flew uphill out of the canyon bottom.

I saw a similar chase two years later, this time in mid-August, once again in South Fork. Once again a male Eared Trogon fled before the onslaught of a male Elegant. And again it flew out of the streambed riparian up a steep slope into a conifer forest.

It seems possible that Elegant Trogons exclude Eared Trogons from the major canyons in Arizona's border ranges, at least from May through July. As Elegants fledge their young and migrate south into Mexico from August through November, Eared Trogons sightings become increasingly common.

In 1977, food competition probably existed between the Eared Trogons and American Robins, Hermit Thrushes, Northern Flickers, Red-naped Sapsuckers, and Acorn Woodpeckers, all of which foraged on madrone berries. Robins were by far the most numerous birds in South Fork, and the clamor of their calling was audible long before I reached the madrone groves. However, Eared Trogons were apparently the dominant species among these opportunists; while robins were very common in adjacent trees, they seldom fed in a madrone occupied by an Eared Trogon. Nor did I witness any other species attempting to drive the trogons away.

Rose Ann Rowlett watched Eared Trogons, Mexican Trogons, and Aztec Thrushes feeding in the same madrone trees in Durango, Mexico. The only interaction she observed there was when an Aztec Thrush chased off American Robins on two separate occasions.

Habitat:
How to Find an Eared Trogon

No one knows how many Eared Trogons exist in Arizona. Many have speculated that the quartet of trogons—two adults and two young of the year—discovered back in 1977, actually represented a successful U.S. breeding effort in the Chiricahua Mountains. On August 11, 1979, I found a subadult male two miles above the road head in South Fork. Subsequent sightings in the intervening years are generally vague when it comes to age—or even gender. The immature plumages of Eared Trogons have yet to appear in any field guide. Because most observers have teethed their identification skills on Elegant Trogons, all trogons with iridescent green backs and red breasts are apt to be considered males.

But the two paramount reasons we know so little about Eared Trogons are temporal and spatial. They apparently nest between August and October, well after most birders visit the southeastern Arizona sky islands.

Early autumn is the most productive time of the entire year in the borderland region, alive with ripening fruits and with the insects that materialize after the rains of July and August. When the monsoons end in mid-September, an Indian summer of mild, clear days prevails for one to two months before the first hard frosts. Eared Trogons fledge their young in this interlude.

The second reason is that Eared Trogons live in the cliff-walled upper reaches of the canyons beyond where all roads end, an area of rugged terrain that most birders never penetrate. With a handful of exceptions, all Eared Trogon sightings since their discovery in 1977 have occurred in Arizona's three most visited birdwatching sites: South Fork Cave Creek, Ramsey Canyon, and Madera Canyon. These reports probably tell us more about where birders do their birding than about where Arizona's Eared Trogons actually occur.

Eared Trogons in Mexico are birds of conifer forests between 6,000 and 10,000 feet elevation. In Mexico, they are associated with the barrancas, river canyons with sheer rock faces that rise in tiers to the plateaus that cap the Sierra Madre. Where I have often watched them near Creel in the state of Chihuahua, they are typically on the canyon terraces 100 feet or higher above the valley floor. The elevation of the Río Cusárare here is between 7,500 and 8,000 feet above sea level.

The areas where Eared Trogons have been found in Arizona are remarkably similar to the Sierra Madre. Not only do they share many of the same tree species, they also have tremendous cliffs that resemble the barranca rimrock of Mexico. This headwater region of the major canyons of the Chiricahua, Huachuca, and Santa Rita Mountains is simply too rough for roads; in fact, the high country of all three mountains is now protected from future road incursion as part of our national wilderness system.

The trails that thread these defiles are extremely steep. Understandably, traffic by birdwatchers is light. Likely canyons where Eared Trogons could be expected—drainages such as Price and Rucker in the Chiricahuas—go entirely unvisited by birders in most years. Even upper South Fork Cave Creek, the single most popular destination for those seeking an Elegant Trogon, is seldom checked for its larger relative. Few go beyond Maple Camp, 1.7 miles above the trail head. After 3.5 miles, the trail climbs out of the main canyon and follows a dry branch another 4.0 miles and 2,500 feet of switchbacks up to the Chiricahua Crest Trail. To reach this junction via the Crest Trail is 7.5 miles—one way. Yet, this is the elevational zone where Eared Trogons could be expected to occur.

Compounding the difficulty, no man-made trail actually continues up the main canyon of South Fork Cave Creek. Only shallow depressions show where generations of Black Bears have stepped in the tracks of their predecessors as they navigate through the ant-infested willow thickets, forming a path that crisscrosses the wilderness stream. Ledges of sheer rhyolite and the presence of living water should make the main canyon attractive to Eared Trogons. Yet, most years, neither biologist nor birder penetrates upper South Fork Cave Creek.

Even if there were roads and trails into the canyon heads of the border ranges, we have no assurance that Eared Trogon sightings would increase. Remember, Joe T. Marshall found Eared Trogons using ridge tops during his surveys of the northern Sierra Madre in the 1950s. Rose Ann Rowlett described the area in Durango where she found the birds as "probably the continental divide—an area of moist pine-oak forest with mosses, ferns, epiphytes, and gurgling mountain streams. Here, at 8,600 feet, Douglas fir became predominant in the shaded canyons and slopes . . .".

Unlike Elegant Trogons, which are apparently ecologically tied to streamside woodlands at the northern limits of their range, *Euptilotis* seems to prefer the conifer forest above the canyon floor. Competition may be another factor. It may be no coincidence that the preponderance of all Eared Trogon sightings in Arizona come in autumn, after virtually all Elegant Trogons have deserted the canyons for warmer climates.

Alternatively, an autumnal descent to stream bottoms may simply be part of the Eared Trogon's annual cycle. In addition to greater food potential in the canyons at this time of year, possibly the lower elevations offer Eareds shelter from cold nights in the high country. If young have been successfully fledged, the riparian forest may also afford them better cover from avian predators like the Northern Goshawk. Or, a descent into the lower canyons may be preliminary to migration to Mexico for the winter.

While a few Elegant Trogons overwinter in Arizona nearly every year, primarily in the lower elevation Atascosa Mountains, the overwhelming majority leave the U.S. If short-winged Elegants can make this annual passage, there is little doubt Eared Trogons could follow a similar route. We do know, however, that one pair of Eareds passed the winter of 1991-92 in the high Huachuca Mountains. Odds are good Eared Trogons spend little time, even in the fall, in the lower canyons reached by both roads and birders. The likelihood is that Arizona's Eared Trogons live in cliff-walled headwater forests miles above the nearest roads. As Robert Morse wrote in 1987:

> Only one who has never seen the Chiricahuas could doubt that Eared Trogons could be nesting within a mile or two of the South Fork trail and remain undetected . . . The mountains are rugged and extensive, the trails are few, and birders cover only a fraction of them.

1991 was a banner year for the U.S. population of Eared Trogons. By late August, the number of Eared Trogons reported from southern Arizona led the Southwest regional reports editors of *American Birds* to conclude that no less than eight, and possibly as many as 12, adults were present. Remember, those figures only reflect Eareds that were actually seen, all below 7,000 feet, all on the periphery of correct habitat. I agree with those who believe the true population in 1991 was no less than 12 Eared Trogons. I've got a hunch there may have been as many as 20.

Nest

After years of observing Eared Trogons in the Barranca del Cobre region of western Chihuahua, I finally found a pair feeding young in a nest hole on September 4, 1990. Their cavity was approximately 70 feet up a partially dead 95-foot-tall Mexican White Pine. Judging from the hole's appearance, the trogons were using an abandoned Northern Flicker nest situated at the division between living and dead wood.

The tree itself was located at the "corner" of two canyons where a major tributary entered the Río Cusárare, perhaps 150 feet above the confluence, midway between the valley floor and the rimrock above. A large living branch with a few sprays of pine needles provided a convenient perch for the adults before they entered the nest with food. Elevation of the nest tree was about 7,800 feet.

Ponderosa pine is the dominant conifer here, but other Mexican White pines, Chihuahua Pine, and Weeping Pine grow on the same slope. Douglas fir, Arizona cypress, Texas madrone, and a handful of aspen follow the winding course of the Río Cusárare. As of 1993, this nest has been home for Eared Trogon nestlings during the first week of September for four consecutive years.

The adult Eared Trogons on the Río Cusárare have always proven incredibly shy. All summer the children of the Tarahumara Indians tend their parents' goats and sheep along the river while their mothers keep the household and their fathers cultivate small plots of corn. The kids have to rustle their own meals while they're out, and the big, brightly painted trogons must offer tempting targets for their slings. Perhaps that explains in part why Eared Trogons on the Río Cusárare disappear from the vicinity of their nest while my groups are still over 200 yards away.

Sheri Williamson, co-manager of The Arizona Nature Conservancy's Ramsey Canyon Preserve, observed the same behavior at the first known U.S. nest of *Euptilotis neoxenus* in October, 1991. In an article for *Winging It*, the monthly newsletter of the American Birding Association, she wrote, "Though both parents were wary, the male showed extreme nervousness at the presence [at the nest] of up to a dozen admirers at a time." Through Williamson's prompt action, a cadre of responsible southern Arizona birdwatchers was organized to document and protect the Eared Trogon nest in Ramsey Canyon.

That was no easy task. Birders seldom visit the area above "the Box," a slot no more than 20 feet wide cut by Ramsey Creek through a 200-foot-thick stratum of Precambrian rock. To protect a relict population of endangered Lemon Lilies, the Arizona Nature Conservancy has wisely closed the Box to the public. Access to upper Ramsey from the Preserve requires a steep 2¼-mile hike that includes ascending a half mile series of tortuous switchbacks. The first Arizona nest of Eared Trogon was discovered another half mile upstream from the Box at about 6,700 feet elevation, 1,300 feet above the Ramsey Visitor Center.

Eared Trogons were videotaped entering a Northern Flicker cavity 29 feet high in a dead bigtooth maple October 10. The tree was about 75 feet above the canyon floor. On October 12, both adults were observed feeding young by a small group of fortunate birders. After confirming the report and actually hearing the baby trogons begging food, Sheri mounted a group of volunteers that monitored the nest for the final two weeks of October 1991.

My turn came October 28, two days after a brief but frigid storm blew through the Huachuca Mountains. I had a worrisome premonition when I saw the male and heard both birds calling just above the Box and well away from their nest. Al and Beth Morgan had seen the male bring food to the nest early that morning, but it flew away with the food still in its bill. Neither bird came to the nest during my watch. That afternoon I told Sheri I thought the nest had failed. On October 30, volunteers from the Bisbee Fire Department climbed the nest tree and confirmed the worst.

Two dead chicks were retrieved from the cavity. One was badly decomposed and had evidently died earlier, but one was covered with black and yellow down and seemed well fed. It had apparently succumbed to hypothermia during the storm. Amongst the debris at the bottom of the unlined chamber was a feather from a Northern Flicker, evidence of how the cavity was created. The chamber measured 5½ inches in diameter and 11 inches deep.

Williamson speculates in her *Winging It* article that the Eared Trogons delayed nesting in 1991 because of heavy pressure from birders. If true, a least one youngster froze to death because the adults were dodging listers when they should have been choosing a cavity.

> Though we will never know for certain, the evidence strongly suggests that the intense human activity in the upper canyon between mid-August and Labor Day discouraged the birds from settling down to nest. But whether the nest failure was ultimately the result of the unethical and inconsiderate behavior of a few visitors, the sheer numbers of people in the upper canyon, or factors beyond our control, it is sobering to consider the negative impact that birding and other nonconsumptive outdoor recreation can have on wildlife of all kinds.

Eared Trogons have had 15 years to acclimate to their new home in the United States. It is clear that, to insure the survival of these fabulous birds from the Sierra Madre, every effort must be made to protect them from excessive human attention. But it also seems true that a small population of these rare and beautiful birds have established residence in our border ranges.

If only we conduct ourselves ethically, the royal red, blue, and emerald Eared Trogon may grace the mountain highlands of southeastern Arizona for years to come.

Literature Consulted

Balda, R. P. 1965. The birds of the Chiricahua Mountains, Arizona. Unpublished doctoral dissertation, University of Illinois, Chicago.

La Bastille, A., Allen, D. G. , and Durrell, L. W. 1972. Behavior and feather structure of the Quetzal. *Auk* 89:339-348.

Dunn, J. L. 1983. Field Guide to the Birds of North America. National Geographic Society, Washington. Pages 232-3.

Morse, R. J. 1987. Mystery bird of the Chiricahuas. *Birding* 19:5:16-20.

Peterson, R. T. and Chalif, E. L. 1973. *A Field Guide to Mexican Birds.* Houghton Mifflin Company. Boston. Page 109, Plate 21.

Ridgway, R. 1911. The birds of North and Middle America: Part V. United States National Museum Bulletin 50. Pages 732-742.

Skutch, A. F. 1944. Life history of the Quetzal. *Condor* 46:213-235.

Williamson, S. 1992. First nesting of Eared Trogon in the United States. *Winging It* 4:7:1-4.

Zimmerman, D. A. 1978. Eared Trogon—immigrant or visitor? *American Birds* 32:135-139.

About the Author

A former employee of both the National Park Service and the U.S. Forest Service, Richard Cachor Taylor began an eight-year-long research project into the life history, ecology, and conservation of the Elegant Trogon in 1976. In 1977, Taylor reported the first Eared Trogon ever seen in the United States. The July, 1979 issue of *Audubon Magazine* called him "Arizona's resident trogon expert."

He is also the author of *Hiking Trails & Wilderness Routes of the Chiricahua Mountains* (1977). While teaching environmental studies and wilderness problems for Cochise College, Taylor founded Borderland Tours, a company dedicated to providing educational birdwatching and natural history trips.